The WATER GARDEN

THE WAYSIDE GARDENS COLLECTION

The WATER GARDEN

A Practical Guide to Planning & Planting

Peter Robinson

John E. Elsley, General Editor for The Wayside Gardens Collection

Sterling Publishing Co., Inc. New York

Library of Congress Cataloging-in-Publication Data

Robinson, Peter, 1938–
　　The water garden : a practical guide to planning & planting / by
Peter Robinson.
　　　　p.　　cm.　—　(The Wayside Gardens collection)
　　Includes index.
　　ISBN 0-8069-0845-9
　　1. Water gardens.　I. Title.　II. Series.
SB423.R583　1995
635.9′674—dc20
94–31830
CIP

2 4 6 8 10 9 7 5 3 1

Published 1995 by Sterling Publishing Company, Inc.
387 Park Avenue South, New York, N.Y. 10016

The Wayside Gardens Collection edition

© 1995 Conran Octopus Limited
The original edition first published
in Great Britain by Conran Octopus Limited
37 Shelton Street, London WC2H 9HN
Text and original planting schemes © 1994 by Peter Robinson
Design and layout © 1994 Conran Octopus Limited
Distributed in Canada by Sterling Publishing
℅ Canadian Manda Group, One Atlantic Avenue, Suite 105
Toronto, Ontario, Canada M6K 3E7
Printed and bound in Hong Kong
All Rights Reserved

American Project Editor	Hannah Steinmetz
Project Editor	Jane O'Shea
Project Art Editor	Ann Burnham
Editors	Carole McGlynn
	Caroline Davison
Designer	Lesley Craig
Picture Researcher	Helen Fickling
Production	Julia Golding
Illustrators	Lynn Chadwick
	David Ashby
	Vanessa Luff
	Valerie Price

Sterling ISBN 0-8069-0845-9

FRONT JACKET Nymphaea *'Masaniello.'*

BACK JACKET *The luxuriant growth of astilbes, iris and* Gunnera manicata *brings color to this well-placed pool in summer.*

PAGE 1 *Dense, informal planting complements a beautiful reflective pool, broken by a curtain of water from a wall fountain.*

PAGE 2 *Sunlight catches a perfectly sited water lily in this informal woodland pool.*

RIGHT *Weathered boulders enhance this shallow stream, blending with the water forget-me-not* (Myosotis scorpioides) *and the hostas.*

CONTENTS

THE INFLUENCE
OF WATER

Water has made an important impact on gardens since aquatic plants were first cultivated by the great Asiatic cultures for their medicinal uses, their aesthetic appeal and their religious connotations. The spread of the great empires extended artistic cultures into new continents, and the characteristic styles of historical water landscapes still make their mark on contemporary designs. New materials and technology allow the modern water garden to capture in miniature the bold, traditional designs of former centuries or to distill elements of them in simple water features valued for their tranquil qualities in today's bustling world.

A simple fountain adds sparkle and movement to a small space, heavy with the scent of roses, forming a perfect retreat in which to relax. The arched jets of water make an exuberant contrast to the formality of the geometrically clipped hedges.

Water provides such a variety of contrasting moods that there are few garden styles which would not be improved by its inclusion. Whether the need is for bustling noise and movement or for stillness and reflection, water is one of the most rewarding elements to use in a garden. The sound of moving water cools down the hottest of days and sharpens every sound on the stillest. Falling water conveys exhilaration as it pounds over rocky waterfalls, refreshment as it splashes into fountain saucers and relaxation as it gently babbles over pebbles and stones. In contrast, completely still water induces contemplation. Nowhere in a garden is the siting of a seat more appropriate, allowing reflection to prompt a daydream, a memory or an idea. The influence of a water garden in fact extends well beyond the water's edge. Even in the most formal design its presence can heighten the appreciation of color and balance in a garden, providing a focus to a symmetrical composition. In an informal garden water nourishes the lush surroundings of a pool, extending the opportunity to use moisture-loving plants whose turgid vigor lasts throughout the driest of summers.

The attraction of water is by no means limited to a large garden. There is a role for water in the smallest of spaces, whether it is the home for a pygmy water lily shading a pet goldfish in a balcony tub, or a series of small cascades spilling into a patio pool. Its presence has an undeniable appeal, sometimes therapeutic, often stimulating. While a water garden enhances its surroundings, it is also, in many ways, a self-contained world: a source of constant and intriguing interest where the naturalist can study the myriad tiny creatures hardly visible to the naked eye, a unique space for the gardener to exploit a specialist group of plants and a private place in which to think or dream, allowing water's restful qualities to soothe and soften any noise and discord beyond the garden. The fascination of underwater life, often such a magnet in childhood, still plays an important part in the attraction of water. The incentive for creating a pond may well stem from the desire to observe the darting movements of submerged creatures in

crystal-clear water, as well as that of diverse insects and amphibians.

The creation of a water garden should not be an impulse decision; never be tempted to buy a self-assembly kit for instant installation without considering the long-term effects. Modern technology has provided the construction materials and equipment which enable a water garden to be built in a fraction of the time once required, but such speedy installation has all too often resulted in an algae-ridden pool sitting awkwardly in its surroundings, spoiling rather than enhancing valuable outdoor space. Since a water feature is more difficult to change than a group of herbaceous plants, the siting and the choice of materials require a great deal of thought, as we shall see. A successful water garden, whose style, siting, construction and planting have all been given careful consideration, will amply reward the owner with surprising changes on each visit.

The mechanically minded gardener can have a constant challenge in the water garden. The pump section of aquatic centers bears testimony to the

LEFT *The noise of moving water is exploited with great mastery at Shute House by Sir Geoffrey Jellicoe, a leading contemporary landscape architect. A series of waterfalls using ridge tiles as spouts creates a cacophony of sounds.*

ABOVE RIGHT *A perfect combination of reflection and planting is achieved in this large pool, where the water lilies punctuate the water's surface, providing interest and welcome shade to submerged life. The midsummer sunshine is captured in the foreground, shining through the foliage.*

BELOW *A seat is well placed beside a lush formal pool, alive with the movement of fish and insects. Perfectly secluded, and with the pool margins planted with moisture-loving plants, such as astilbes and hostas, a natural harmony exists of water and surroundings.*

potential offered by moving water for the budding hydraulic engineer. The hardware of water gardening is big business, not only in the supply of an ever-increasing variety of efficient pumps, but in the endless gadgetry, the changing fountain lights and the range of jets, filters and valves.

Above all, the water garden is a haven for the plant enthusiast. From water lilies to moisture-loving trees, the scope for assembling a specialist plant collection or designing a harmonious mix is enormous. The rapid rate of growth of aquatic plants enables seedlings to become luxuriant specimens in the space of a few months. From the smallest leaves of floating plants to the large, dramatic leaves of *Gunnera* and *Rheum*, the water garden is a canvas for all types of growth, from delicate to lush.

Whatever the initial reason for including water in the garden, there is great satisfaction in completing a pool where good design, sound construction and appropriate choice of plants have been brought together to create a composition in which a different reflection can be seen with every change in the sky.

An opulent fountain in the grand style at Versailles forms a magnificent and noisy center point in a garden of clipped hedges and long, straight canal-like pools. The elaborate construction of such a fountain and the detail in the design provide a perfect contrast to the simplicity of formal planting.

Water gardens in history

The inclusion of water in the garden is by no means a recent phenomenon. Water has always enhanced the world's gardens, particularly in countries with hot, dry climates where it is treated with great respect. The early use of water to enrich the pleasures of a garden through symbols is well documented. In the paradise gardens of Islam, the early Persian gardens were divided into four by formal water canals which intersected in the center to symbolize the rivers of life. Along the length of the canals and at their intersection, arching jets of water were created, using pressure from the water's source on higher ground.

These designs were copied by other Muslims after their conquest of Persia in the seventh century. And early in the eighth century, when the Muslim Arabs invaded Spain, their love of and skill in the use of water went with them, and they created many beautiful courtyard gardens such as those seen in the Alhambra and Generalife in Granada, with their canals and fountains. The Persian concept of water being essential to the pleasure of a courtyard garden was repeated with great skill through the centuries.

The Islamic tradition in the use of water, so well exploited in Spain by the Moors, was further developed in the sixteenth-century Moghul gardens in India. The Moghuls used the hillsides of northern India to create sophisticated waterfalls in gardens where the sound of water had more importance than in the quieter Islamic gardens. In mastering the formal use of moving water, they developed huge cascades where large volumes of foaming or effervescent water created very fine sprays in which rainbows could be seen in certain lights. One of their most outstanding formal water gardens was created around the Taj Mahal, where water lilies were magnificently displayed in this quiet and awe-inspiring setting.

Farther east, in China, genius of a different style made use of water in gardens for nearly two thousand years. The Chinese gardens were designed to imitate in miniature their country's natural landscape, with its expansive lakes and inlets. Lakes contained islands and graceful, semi-circular bridges were positioned to create beautiful reflected images. Similarly, Japan's gardens always symbolized a deep reverence of nature, where water played such an integral part that it was simulated by sand or stones in situations where it was impractical to introduce water itself. Stones or rocks might suggest the course of a stream, and sand or gravel raked into concentric outlines may represent the natural ripples of a pool.

In more recent history, gardens created on the grand scale, particularly in Europe, have embodied much of the detail of the early Persian water gardens. While Italy is renowned for its fountains and cascades, many of the French gardens make maximum use of canals, in gardens like those of Versailles, for instance. There are few renowned gardens, historical or contemporary, that have not used water to enhance the strength of a bold symmetrical design or the freedom of an informal planting.

The cooling effect of fountains, particularly when backlit by sunshine, is perfectly illustrated here in the Patio de la Azequia at the Generalife in Granada, Spain. The Islamic tradition of using water in straight canals is fully expressed in this courtyard, where even on the hottest of days, the splash of the arching fountains exerts a refreshing and cooling influence.

THE DESIGN OF
THE WATER GARDEN

Water is a welcome ingredient of any garden, large or small, formal or informal; it will enhance both traditional or modern styles in country or town. Imaginative designers use its unique properties in an increasing variety of situations, made possible by the advent of new materials and a greater awareness of the impact of water in small spaces. A water feature in a garden does not have to be restricted to a static body of water in a square, circle, rectangle or kidney shape. Water has a unique freedom, whether it is splashing from a wall spout, bursting from a fountain jet, lapping over an obstruction or reflecting a slender segment of sky in a narrow, canal-like pool.

Forming the perfect medium to heighten the symmetry of the formal garden, this simple pool devoted to water lilies is sufficiently restrained to allow reflection to be fully exploited. The seat set against a yew hedge is framed by a pair of shaped catalpas, balanced by precisely placed pots of Agapanthus.

Siting a water feature

PLANTS FOR
REFLECTION

For a small garden:

Abies koreana

Acer palmatum
   (Japanese maple)

Alnus incana 'Aurea'
   (yellow-leaved alder)

For the larger garden:

Cortaderia selloana
   (pampas grass)

Corylus avellana
   'Contorta'
   (twisted hazel)

Gunnera manicata

Metasequoia
   glyptostroboides
   (dawn redwood)

Pyrus salicifolia

Rheum palmatum

Water is such a continuous source of interest that any water feature should be sited where it will have maximum impact. In deciding where to include water, sit for a while in the garden and imagine where movement, noise or reflection could add a new dimension to the pleasure of the garden. There is a real bonus to any water feature which can be seen easily from the house, but in certain cases this may not be important. Wildlife pools, for instance, may require part of the pool to be hidden from view to encourage shy creatures to come to it. And there is a pleasant element of surprise in discovering a hidden pool, in a garden divided into distinct "rooms."

There are several considerations to bear in mind when choosing a site. These are in part aesthetic and in broad terms concern matching a formal or informal water feature to the style of the garden (see pages 18–23). But you will also need to consider the practical aspects of the site, such as the lay of the land, the proximity of trees and the general microclimate, as well as the question of services to your water feature. Electricity may be required for pumps, heating or lighting, and if the proposed site is some distance from its nearest source, you should consider the cost of taking power to the poolside. Similarly, in water gardens where frequent topping off from the domestic water supply is necessary, it is wise to ensure that this is reasonably close. Always check that the pool excavation will not damage any existing water pipes, electric cables or drains before starting the construction. In most gardens, the presence of manholes will indicate where the soil pipes are, but in a large old garden there may be no such clues and you should excavate with caution.

The value of reflection

The reflective qualities of water are one of its most attractive and pleasurable aspects. If the pool can be sited near the house, the reflections will be most varied and even relatively small changes in the viewing height—sitting as against standing, for instance—will subtly alter the reflective picture.

While viewing the garden from a favorite chair, try to imagine any possible reflections or background features which the future pool will highlight. If there is no particular merit in the existing features for reflection, this is an ideal opportunity to plant a striking specimen plant which will be reflected in years to come once the pool is built (suggestions are given in the list on the left). In a larger garden there will be opportunity to plant taller trees some distance from the pond; these will be reflected as they mature.

Water plays such an important part in the overall design of a garden that its role as a hub to other features may preclude it from being sited in the best position when viewed from the house. This is especially so in a formal garden, where the pool has to be sited where it will act as a pivot to balance the symmetrical features. In an informal garden, with a less rigid design, it will be easier to place the pool to make the most of its reflective qualities.

Positioning the pool

Of the various practical aspects to be considered when choosing the best site for your pool (shown on page 16), the garden contours are one of the most important. You should check carefully the slope of the proposed site to ensure that there is no danger of surrounding land flooding or draining into the pool. It is vital to have a stable ecological and chemical balance in any pool to sustain clear water and a healthy environment for pond life. Any risk of flooding must be kept to an absolute minimum, as a sudden introduction of nutrients, through dissolved or partially dissolved fertilizer, could upset this balance for some time. This is only likely to occur if the pool is positioned in a low-lying area or at the bottom of a large, sloping lawn, in areas prone to frequent and heavy downpours. In such a case, it may be necessary to install drains, running to a nearby soakaway (stone-filled drainage hole), to intercept surface water after downpours. But if these are rare, you may consider their harmful effects to be outweighed by other, more favorable aspects which make the proposed site suitable. Another important factor relating to the level of a future pool is the water table of the land, or the depth at which water is found when a hole is dug. In winter this is often a few inches higher than in the summer, and on certain very heavy soil types it may be quite near the surface. The pressure of a high water table can cause a flexible liner to billow near the pool's surface. Dig a trial hole in winter 1½–2 ft. deep, and if it fills with water higher than 1 ft., you may have a problem. The presence of a high water table does not preclude you from using the proposed site, but it is advisable to see if the excavated area can be drained to a nearby outlet beforehand. If there is no outlet for a drain, the area should be connected by a drainpipe to a soakaway which is lower than the proposed water level of the new pond.

By using a submersible pump in the soakaway whenever it is full, the water can be drained to the nearest outlet. An alternative remedy would be to excavate the waterlogged soil and create a slightly raised pond above the water table, using the excavated material around the sides. The hole created below the water table can then be backfilled with rubble or gravel under a covering of soil.

If neither of these two remedies is possible, and there is no alternative to siting the pond in a wet hollow, a one-way valve can be fitted into a flexible synthetic-rubber liner. This allows the water to enter the liner from below, under pressure from the water table, but prevents the escape of water from the pool if and when the water table falls. Such valves are best fitted by an experienced contractor.

Levels and landscaping

A sloping site should not deter you from installing a water feature, provided this is taken into account. In a formal garden, any changes in level throughout the plot may be enhanced by retaining walls, creating a series of flat areas, which allow a pool to be integrated at any of the levels. In an informal garden, the undulating or sloping site affords scope for water to

be used on several levels at once. The siting of a pool is still critical, as water could look unnatural if it is sited on a ridge or at the top of a slope. Although the lowest point may seem to be the obvious site for a solitary pool, the problems of flooding or of a high water table, described earlier, may mean that the pool has to be elevated, where it can also be siphoned out if there is any need to empty it. Informal pools can be satisfactorily integrated into a slope, provided the length of the pool follows the contours of sloping land as closely as possible. This is best achieved by a gentle cut-and-fill method of construction where some of the soil dug out of the original slope is gently mounded on the lower side of the pool and later stabilized by creeping plants such as *Calla*, *Peltandra* and, on larger schemes, *Darmera*.

Water seems to sit naturally in a woodland glade and this naturalistic area of a garden forms the ideal position to create an informal pool. The shade cast by the adjacent trees would limit the planting in the water and water lilies should be avoided in this kind of site.

The sloping, informal site affords an excellent opportunity to create a stream which links a series of small pools by waterfalls. This can be done even in a small garden—the water channels between pools need be no longer than 1–2 ft. to be effective. This is one of the most exciting ways of using water on a sloping site, particularly where rock can be incorporated and the edges of the streams and rock pools can be planted.

Frost pockets

Frost pockets are areas of low-lying land which collect cold air. The effects of siting a pool in a frost pocket are that the water cools down and freezes more rapidly, increasing the danger of frost damage to certain plants. While this is not a problem for most hardy aquatics, it would be sensible to avoid such a position where you plan to grow plants with early spring flowers, such as the skunk cabbage (*Lysichiton americanus*), or with frost-tender foliage, such as *Gunnera manicata*.

Shade

The amount and type of shade the pool will receive has a marked influence on the planting—water lilies, for instance, need all the sunshine they can get. Dappled shade from nearby trees which lasts for only a few hours is the least damaging type of shade for aquatic plants, particularly as deciduous trees cast

hardly any shade in early-spring, when the water requires warming up. Shade from buildings is more harmful, and if you are considering locating the pool near the house it is important to know how much shade the house, or other buildings, casts at different times of year and for how long in the day. The more hours of direct sun in spring and summer, the better the plants will grow and flower. But if all other considerations favor a site where shade is the only limiting factor, you could choose shade-loving plants or have a reflective or fountain pool, unplanted.

Trees

The effect of siting a pool near to trees will depend on the orientation and proximity of certain tree species and the size of the water feature. There are a number of excellent trees that are tolerant of wet soil, like the dawn redwood (*Metasequoia glyptostroboides*) and yellow-leaved alder (*Alnus incana* 'Aurea'), which will enhance a nearby pool, allowing lovely reflections every season. Certain moisture-loving species of willow (*Salix*) which are cut back hard each spring are also acceptable close to water as their foliage canopy is not allowed to become excessive.

Always avoid sites under trees with a heavy canopy of large, deciduous leaves since the leaf canopy not only shades the pool heavily but also pollutes the water when the leaves fall into it, then sink to the bottom and decompose. If the autumn leaf fall is not

The hedge and surrounding shrubby planting pampers and provides essential wind protection in this exposed countryside site. The trees are sufficiently distant to provide the first line of protection from wind without shading the pool. Shelter belts like trees provide the optimum protection at 7–10 times their height on the leeward side of the planting. The softer herbaceous planting like the astilbes in the foreground take full advantage of the less turbulent air.

Drawing up a siting plan

On a scale plan of your garden, mark the house, the main viewing windows, the boundaries and any drain manholes. Indicate the orientation, wind direction and the main slope. Plot in any plant features which will influence the siting of the pool and the area of shade they cast, as well as any specimens worthy of reflection. Take a piece of paper or card, cut roughly to the shape and scale of the proposed pool, and move it around the garden until you find the position where it can best be seen and enjoyed, avoiding shade and wind.

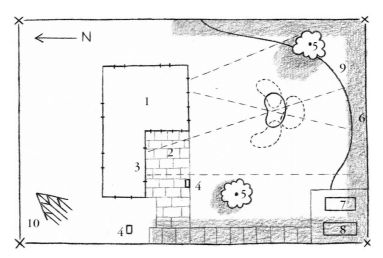

This plan is taken a stage further in planning the planting (see page 70).

 1 *House*
 2 *Patio*
 3 *Patio window*
 4 *Manhole*
 5 *Tree*
 6 *Shade from boundaries*
 7 *Compost*
 8 *Shed*
 9 *Border*
10 *Main wind direction*

Wind

A windy site spoils the appearance of surface-leaved plants like water lilies by disturbing the water. As wind causes the spray of fountains to drift, it restricts their use, particularly fountains with a fine spray pattern. A solid windbreak such as a wall or solid fence causes the wind to eddy, creating gusts elsewhere, so the best solution for a windbreak is planting, which filters the wind rather than forming a solid barrier. Hedges make a good windbreak in formal gardens and mixed-shrub planting in informal gardens; they should be planted far enough away from the pool to avoid casting shade. The calming effect of adjacent planting in reducing the wind speed can be felt for some distance on the leeward side of the plants; bear in mind when choosing and siting a windbreak planting that the optimum reduction is felt at 7–10 times the height of the windbreak.

Safety

Whatever style of water garden you choose, it is vital to make the feature as safe as possible. Where the marginal shelves (see page 46) run around most of the pool perimeter, they can be used to support a grid or mesh a few inches below the water surface, covering the central deeper zone. But it is important to remember that a toddler can drown in only a few inches of water, and the idea of a water garden may have to be abandoned by parents of young children until they are older, because the precautions necessary to make the pool totally safe can negate its aesthetic value.

There is similar concern for safety when electricity is introduced to water for submersible pumps or lighting, since water and electricity can be a lethal mix. No matter how simple the installation may appear, it is important to use approved electrical fittings and equipment and to consult or, better still, to employ a qualified electrician. As an extra precaution, it is strongly recommended that you install a contact circuit breaker where electrical power voltage equipment is used in or near the water. These devices are simple to connect and, in the event of any electricity leakage, they cut off the current within 30 milliseconds to protect against severe electric shock.

prevented from sinking to the pool bottom, by netting or frequent raking off, the leaves eventually form a black sludge which discharges harmful methane gas into the water. Certain trees are particularly toxic to plant and animal life in the water: these include yew *(Taxus)*, holly *(Ilex)* and *Laburnum*. Conifers shed their leaves continuously, spoiling the surface with dusty needles and bud scales.

Tree roots may cause damage when they are in close proximity to pools. In natural or puddled ponds, the invading roots of large trees not only break the compacted seal of clay, but also draw up a considerable volume of water in high summer, which causes a drop in the water level. In pools made with a flexible liner, the smallest of hairline cracks in the liner will be exploited by the tree's fine root hairs.

Choosing the best water feature

There are many ways of introducing moving or still water into a garden, whether traditional or modern, large or small. Water's versatility allows it to fit into any garden style, so the type of water feature can be chosen primarily to suit the needs of the owner, though there are certain considerations that make particular features more appropriate to the style of a formal or an informal garden.

Formal pools

Formal pools have a distinct geometric shape, usually a square, a rectangle or a circle. There are several other variations, such as a semi-circle adjacent to a wall, or more complex ones such as a series of interlocking circles and rectangles. Formal pools fit best into an existing formal garden with straight paths, clipped hedges and symmetrically balanced planting, or into a formal part of a garden, such as a terrace or a regularly shaped lawn. Pools fitting into this style usually have a paved surround.

Long, canal-like pools can work well in the modern garden and have as soothing an influence as those seen in the Moorish gardens of Spain. They can link features and enhance a focal point, seemingly adding length to a garden. Such an illusion of greater space is particularly valuable in the small city garden, where the reflected light in the water can relieve the claustrophobic effect of high walls or surrounding buildings.

Formal pools allow great scope for reflecting the house when viewed from the garden, particularly if the water is dark in color. A black liner helps to darken the appearance of the water, as does the use of dark colored bricks for any edges under or near the surface. The water level in a formal pool also has a marked influence on its appearance. When full to the brim, the pool's reflective quality and its consequent architectural effect are more dramatic than when there is a gap between the pool surround and the water level. Such a gap is doubled by the reflection, giving the impression that the water is lower than it actually is. The paramount importance of the water level in formal water features highlights the need for

sound construction techniques and adequate topping off facilities (see page 58) for long spells of dry, hot weather.

Formal pools can be raised above ground level and in small city gardens raised pools are particularly useful to maximize light reflection. They not only bring more light to enclosed spaces but display the intriguing qualities of water at a height which can be more fully appreciated by the elderly and disabled. If they are constructed in such a way that their surrounds can be used as a casual seat, this enhances their appeal. The materials used in the construction of the raised walls should blend with the surroundings, be it the walls of the house or any adjacent building or the materials used for the paving.

Changes in levels make a good situation for a raised pool, particularly alongside a flight of steps. Raised pools often provide the opportunity to create waterfalls between pools or canals, and falling water brings sound in addition to movement. At the junction of two levels, a raised pool at the higher level can be linked to a raised pool at the lower level by creating an obstruction, using a large, flat stone on the edge of the top water level. Creating this is more successful in a small formal garden than in an informal situation since an unbroken curtain of water spilling over a flat, square stone is seldom seen in nature and can therefore look contrived in an informal water garden; a babbling effect would be more appropriate in an informal situation.

The number of aquatic plants required in relation to the surface area of water is much smaller in formal pools than in the informal water garden, where there is frequently a background of a bog garden or moisture-loving bed. Planting in formal water also tends to be more architectural: strong, vertical leaves which contrast with the water surface are especially effective, such as the sword-like foliage of irises and the shield-like leaves of pickerel weed *(Pontederia)* and arrowhead *(Sagittaria)*. Long, canal-like pools provide an excellent setting for water lilies. Using several plants of one species or cultivar is more effective in keeping a scheme simple and dramatic.

Iris pseudacorus
A common wild plant and the only yellow-flowered water iris, the flower of the yellow flag was adopted by Louis VII in the fleur de lis, *which he wore in his crusade against the Saracens* ("lis" *being a corruption of* "Louis"). *There are numerous variants in flower color, ranging from white to pale yellow. After pollination by bees, the flowers become attractive, drooping, shiny green seedpods which are much sought after by flower arrangers.*

A weeping pear (Pyrus salicifolia 'Pendula') stands sentinel over this exquisite formal water garden, hidden within mature yew hedges, at Knightshayes in Devon, southwest England. The restrained planting consists of a simple but effective combination of iris and water lily, planted in such a way to allow the statue to be reflected. In an otherwise large, informal garden, the surprise of finding this excellent design, on entering through a small gap in the yew hedge, is even more pleasurable.

Informal pools

Informal pools are irregular in shape with a curving outline giving the appearance of being natural. They fit best into informal gardens with random, more billowing shapes, contours and planting areas, and where any change in level would be left as a natural slope rather than having retaining walls. The edges of the pool can include more than one material, ranging from grass and planting to rocks and cobble stones. Indeed, the perimeter of an informal pool can be softened by planting right up to the water's edge. Informal pools are seldom raised aboveground.

The free shape of an informal water feature should in general be kept simple: too many promontories and fussy curves can destroy the restful qualities of water. Try to achieve proportions that are appropriate to the size of the garden or the surrounding lawn. A tiny pool, for instance, will look ineffective in an expanse of lawn; both its visual appeal and its long-term management will be improved by making it bigger. As informal water has associated plantings near the margins, it is more difficult than formal water to integrate into a very small space. Aim for a minimum of 40 square ft. of surface water in a small garden to enable a satisfactory balance to be achieved within the pool community.

Planting in the informal pool is not limited to submerged and marginal aquatic plants, such as arrowheads (*Sagittaria*) and marsh marigolds (*Caltha*), but can include moisture-loving herbaceous plants such as primulas, rheums and day lilies (*Hemerocallis*), as well as shrubs and small trees for the surrounding area. It would look quite incongruous, however, to create the lush wealth of growth associated with water next to a garden-border planting which is stunted through dry conditions. As the planting boundaries of the informal water garden extend well beyond the water's edge, they require much more room than in the formal water garden, even though the area of clear water surface may be less. The surrounding planting in the different moisture regimes affords great scope for creative

19

plant grouping where texture, form and color add to the appeal of the water surface. Try mixing the bold, plate-like leaves of *Darmera peltata* with the fine, cylindrical stems of *Schoenoplectus lacustris* 'Albescens' and the fiery-red flowers of *Lobelia splendens*. Guidelines on grouping plants together successfully in this rich environment appear in the chapter on Planting and Stocking the Water Garden (see page 63).

The edging around this informal pool is completely masked with a rich variety of planting which blends harmoniously with the woodland background. Primulas and astilbes form the immediate edge, while Japanese maples and mahonia fill the middle ground between the pool and the rest of the garden. Ferns make excellent plants for the moist soil near pool edges, particularly in partially shaded sites.

While a pool with informal edges may seem easier to construct than a formal pool, it is the attention to detail at its margins which helps to make such a pool successful. The sense of space is encouraged where there is hardly any gradient running into the water, suggesting a shallow pool with little or no shadow around the edges. A steep gradient around the pool sides causes more shadow, suggesting greater depth and looking more dangerous.

Streams and waterfalls can create great interest and movement in the informal water garden, using a pump to circulate the water; and making a watercourse is an extremely creative project (see page 52). When executed successfully, with well-chosen and -positioned rocks, streams and waterfalls not only create a landscape in miniature but also provide the opportunity for a wealth of interesting and varied planting along the margins.

A sloping site will provide the opportunity to create a small waterfall as a link between two pools, the base pool at the lower level and the longer, narrower pool, which takes the form of a stream, at the higher level. On a site with a gentle slope, the stream should be designed to meander and vary in width along its length. A more steeply sloping site, while having slight changes in direction, would require only small variations in width on the stretches between the waterfalls. It is a natural temptation in a small, flat garden to use the excavation from the pond to create a mound at its side and to incorporate a waterfall to add interest. But small mounds can very easily look too contrived and are rarely entirely successful.

Wildlife ponds

Wildlife ponds are stocked with native plants, many of which are vigorous and spreading to give cover to shy creatures such as frogs, toads and newts. Their outline is similar to that of an informal pool but would include a shallow beach on part of the pool's perimeter to allow wildlife to move in and out of the water easily. Creatures which hibernate near the water appreciate rocks and stones under which they can hide in the damp soil. Species with dense foliage include flag iris (*Iris pseudacorus*), burr reeds (*Sparganium erectum*) and reedmace (*Typha* species), which provide a source of food and shelter for native fauna. In order to furnish the necessary cover, the foliage must be allowed to remain standing for the duration of the winter rather than being cut down or trimmed.

It may seem at first a contradiction in terms to apply design rules to a pool devoted to wildlife. But while the unplanned pool may successfully perform its role in providing a natural habitat, it could quickly become an overgrown and uncoordinated mess which is out of scale in a small or medium-sized garden. As the attraction of wildlife is the primary objective of wildlife ponds, however, aesthetic considerations must not be allowed to become too dominant a part of the equation.

Wildlife pools would look out of place in the middle of a well-manicured or formal garden. They fit best into larger, well-stocked informal gardens which contain many native plants that act as food reserves for wildlife, such as dog rose *(Rosa canina)*, viburnums, hawthorn *(Crataegus)*, birch *(Betula)*, rowan *(Sorbus)*, primroses *(Primula)* and foxgloves *(Digitalis)*. The grass should not be mown too closely, especially near the edge of the pool, and should preferably contain a mixture of wild flowers which will continue to blossom under an infrequent mowing regime, as long as you have the mower blades set high.

It is advantageous to have part of the pool hidden from view from the house to encourage very timid creatures to gain confidence. If the pool appears to emerge from a plant border, this is a useful method of providing the partially hidden area. As the planting will contain vigorous species such as sweet flag *(Acorus calamus)*, spearwort *(Ranunculus lingua)* and bulrush *(Schoenoplectus lacustris)*, there must be enough space in the garden to accommodate them. If the width of the pool is less than the height of the plants, it will look out of proportion. Aim for a minimum width of one and a half times the height of the tallest plants.

While the use of native plants and minimal cultivation are the hallmarks of wildlife pools, ornamental ponds can still provide wonderful havens for wildlife. Even where exotic or cultivated plants are used, provided they are planted densely in and around an informal pool with some shallow edges, such a water feature will still attract wild creatures.

Container gardens

As the name suggests, these miniature water gardens are confined to containers, making them ideal for small spaces. They generally stand above ground level, or are partially buried and surrounded with rocks to disguise their sides. They fit into either formal or informal styles of garden.

Any non-porous container can be used, provided it has a sufficiently wide mouth. Glazed pots, old stone sinks and stone troughs have all been given a new life as a water feature. The style of the container should blend with the garden. A wooden half-barrel, for instance, will look better than a fiberglass container in a densely planted, informal garden. But where synthetic materials have been used in the garden's

construction, fiberglass can look appropriate, particularly if it is rendered with a texture similar to that of the surrounding surface. Fiberglass also has the advantage of lightness and strength over other materials used for containers.

There are several aquatic plants in scale with a container garden. It helps to keep the water clear if the water surface is partially shaded, and there are some excellent miniature water lilies suitable for tub planting. One little beauty, *Nymphaea* 'Pygmaea Alba,' an ideal hybrid for tub gardens, has small, white, star-shaped flowers, which are scarcely 1½–2 in. across, and dark green, waxy leaves. A pinch of fairy moss *(Azolla caroliniana)* floating on the surface helps to bring an illusion of mystery to the water, and an intriguing plant for near the edges is the miniature reedmace *(Typha minima)*; a relative of the giant reedmaces growing in the margins of

Rocks and the lushness of dense waterside planting makes this pool a haven for wildlife. Many amphibians hibernate under rocks, and where it is easy to scramble onto them from the water, they use the rock surfaces to enjoy brief sessions of sunbathing.

21

large lakes, this species is perfectly miniaturized, with needle-like leaves and small, round, brown flower clusters. The hard edges of tubs look better when softened with plants spilling over their sides; a good example is parrot's feather *(Myriophyllum aquaticum)*, a submerged aquatic whose soft, feathery leaves and curling stems grow out of the water.

Fountain pools

A pool devoted to a fountain makes a striking feature in a garden and must be carefully positioned. A well-designed fountain which is regularly maintained can be the highlight of a garden in which the surrounding planting re-creates the colors and atmosphere of warmer climates. Fountain pools are not normally planted as the water turbulence discourages surface-leaved plants and the constant spray is not conducive to marginal plant growth around the edges. As chemicals often have to be used to eliminate algae from the water, any plants may be weakened by their use.

There are several different types of fountain but they all force water up from the base of a pool, often channeling it through an ornament such as a fish or a nymph, with an orifice such as a mouth. Classical fountain ornaments sometimes contain a series of concentric saucers, with water falling from level to level. Spout fountains have the jets at ground level or a higher level and play the water through several outlets at once. Self-contained fountain units have prefabricated pool bases which stand above ground level or you can construct your own. The proportions of the fountain must sit comfortably within the base pool, which in turn should be in scale with the boundaries of the garden. As a general guideline, the height of a fountain should not be allowed to exceed the radius of the base pool.

Fountains can add a touch of classical formality to a symmetrically balanced garden design. Used as a major focal point, they have considerable impact on the garden. Consider the viewpoint carefully when siting a fountain as the water spray looks best when seen against the sun. A fountain on the south side of a viewpoint is therefore more effective. Keep the background uncluttered, to complement a fountain.

Most good aquatic centers have fountain displays which allow customers to view the performance of the various fountain jet arrangements, and this will help you decide which jet is most appropriate for a particular setting. Do not be tempted to choose a multi-spray jet for an exposed location, as its use will be restricted when it is windy. A single spout from a wide jet will be less vulnerable to drift and the pool will require less topping off. The simplicity of a single-jet spray suits most garden styles far more than a sophisticated spray. Geyser jets have become increasingly popular, providing frothy spouts which are relatively stable in wind. They are quite noisy, however, as they draw in air through small vents to produce the frothiness, and this may make them too obtrusive in a peaceful garden.

Although the performance capacity of a submersible pump (see page 47) may allow several functions, you should resist the temptation to create too many outlets. Pump kits which create both a fountain and waterfall in a small pool may be overdoing the influence of water on the garden. In fountain jets that provide fine spray patterns, maintenance must be of a high order: if algae become established in a fountain pool, the jets soon clog.

Wall fountains Walls provide a good opportunity for a spout of water to spill from an ornamental outlet into a pool underneath. The system requires a submersible pump housed in the base pool that is capable of pumping a sufficient volume of water through a flexible pipe to the spout at the desired height on the wall. This flexible pipe should be

ABOVE *Cherubs make excellent centerpieces for classical fountains in formal settings.*

RIGHT *This shallow fountain saucer needs a high standard of maintenance to keep it in peak condition, and the shallow water will require the addition of algicides to keep it clean.*

BELOW *An old stone container surrounded by gargoyles makes a simple but effective water feature.*

hidden from view, preferably by taking it through a cavity wall or, if possible, behind the wall before returning it through a small hole where the spout will be fixed. An ornamental outlet such as a mask or gargoyle is then connected and secured to the wall. A variety of ornamental spouts for such situations are available at good aquatic centers; they contain a short length of rigid pipe for easy connection to the flexible pipe from the pump.

Semicircular or rectangular raised pools make good base pools, particularly if the sides are of sufficient height and width to sit on. Planting at the back of the pool, using marginals with strong vertical leaves such as iris and *Pontederia*, helps to blend and disguise pipework from the pool to the point of entry in the wall.

Cobblestone fountains

Cobblestone fountains create the sound of water and a pleasing sense of movement without taking up much garden space, so even the most modest of terraces can incorporate such a feature. When turned off, all that is visible is a small area of cobblestones set into the paving; when operating, a small bubbling jet, about 1 ft. high, enhances the color of the cobblestones and brings sound and movement to an area where a pool may not be possible. They require little maintenance and fit equally well into formal or informal gardens, as they have few limitations on their size and shape. The smallest cobblestone fountain requires a surface area approximately 2 ft. × 2 ft. and is best sited near the house. Larger sizes can be constructed using an area 8 ft. × 8 ft., with a spout about 3 ft. high.

Cobblestone fountains make ideal water features near play areas for small children because there is no danger from access to deep water. They also allow water to be used in shady or difficult places where heavy leaf fall or insufficient light would spoil the effectiveness of a more traditional pool.

Aquatic plants grown in containers filled with aquatic compost can be incorporated near the edge of the water feature, hidden in the cobblestones. The large expanse of cobblestones will be softened by plant species such as *Iris pseudacorus* 'Variegata,' *Acorus gramineus* and *Sagittaria sagittifolia*.

INSTALLING A
WATER FEATURE

Before constructing any form of water garden, you need to consider carefully not only the main material to use for the liner but also the many integral factors, both within the pool and beyond its margins, which enhance the fine detail of the finished scheme. These details are best considered at the outset rather than as an afterthought, particularly in informal gardens, where the planting may extend into moisture-loving beds or a bog garden beyond the main pool margin.

This well-constructed split-level raised pool is successfully integrated into the garden by echoing the material of the steps in the pool edge and retaining wall. Bricks turned at right angles form an excellent coping, and the low retaining wall doubles as a seat from which to enjoy the movement of water.

Preformed and flexible pool liners

The basic choice of materials for garden pool construction lies between rigid and flexible liners, and there is a wide range of materials used in the manufacture of each. When visiting the aquatic department of a large garden center, the preformed pools will be the first to catch the eye. Displayed in a wide variety of shapes, sizes and colors, they have an immediate appeal for anyone with limited time to spend on design and construction. The simple circular and rectangular shapes also make good raised or semi-raised pools when their outline is disguised with materials like ornamental stone blocks, bricks, timber or rocks. Raised and semi-raised pools require much less excavation than a ground-level pool and there is less danger of a toddler falling in. The semi-raised pool also offers a degree of frost protection by having its lower part below ground level. But the advent of flexible pool liners, with all their advantages, has had a great impact on the popularity of water gardening, especially for sunken pools.

The decision about which type of liner to use, though fundamental, is only one aspect of building a pool. You should think through the whole project, and everything involved in it, before undertaking any work. All aspects are covered in this chapter but may have to be considered simultaneously—a brief checklist is given on the right.

Preformed pool liners

There are in fact two distinct types of preformed pool: the rigid and the semi-rigid. The rigid type is generally made of resin-bonded fiberglass which has a life expectancy of up to 50 years. These are extremely strong and the material allows them to be molded into complex shapes up to about 13 ft. wide, with shelves at different depths. Many units are designed to interlock and create streams and waterfalls (see page 52). The smaller, semi-rigid pool liners are made in vacuum-formed plastic molds.

Despite the wide range of shapes in preformed pool liners, few make a really practical design for a sunken pool. Many shapes are too fussy, some having narrow-necked areas which are ineffective when installed. With the exception of the stream and waterfall units, which can be used in conjunction with a larger base pool built with a flexible liner, the majority are also too small for a successful garden pool. Many of the units are insufficiently deep, their maximum depth being about 1½ ft.; this is on the borderline of adequate depth for a good balance of fish and plant life in climates where winter temperatures drop below freezing for several weeks.

While ease of installation is one of the advantages of preformed pools, it is vital that the hole into which they are to be fitted is carefully prepared, to ensure even support and to minimize the risk of cracking (see page 32). Once full of water, preformed pools are extremely heavy and great stress is placed on the material if any part is suspended; this applies particularly to the semi-rigid types. The weight of a pool full of water measuring 6 ft. × 6 ft. × 2 ft. deep is over two tons.

Another drawback to their use is the need to disguise their surround when used as an informal pond. Although some types have a flange around the

As there is no water pressure exerted outside a rigid preformed pool, the edging can be entirely decorative without the need for strength. Timber planks have been used to disguise the edges of this preformed, semi-raised pool. Carpeting plants growing in the dry bed adjacent to the preformed pool help to soften the unnatural edging.

BEAR IN MIND
Marginal shelves
These are usually 9–12 in. wide but need to be wider if you intend to make permanent planting beds (see page 46).

Power supply
If you wish to install a pump, pool lighting or a heater, incorporate the cabling during construction.

Overflow or drain pipes
A drain plug and pipework to adjacent drains are only necessary in larger pools housing decorative fish.

Automatic topping-off
This is needed for large fountains with a high evaporation rate that are in constant use. A small water chamber, connected to the main water supply and the fountain pool, is fitted with a ball-cock valve (see page 58).

Pumps
If you are installing any form of moving water, a pump will have to be fitted (see page 47).

Filtration
If the pool is to be stocked with large goldfish, install a filter (see page 50).

A flexible liner has been used to construct this formal, architectural pool, in which the slightly raised brick edging gives greater definition to the pool outline. Where there is no planting to soften the edges of a pool, successful design and construction can only be achieved when there is no liner visible.

top which is intended to represent a paved edge, these look artificial and the best way of disguising them is to lay paving stones on top, which overlap the water (see page 40). Paved edges are acceptable in a formal pool but a better solution in an informal situation would be scrambling plants spilling over the sides into the water. The shape of preformed pools prevents adjacent bog or moisture-loving plants from being grown unless a lined bog area is made alongside it. As the success of an informal pool owes much to planting near the water's edge, the preformed pool is not a good choice here.

Since preformed pool liners are considerably more expensive than flexible pool liners for the same volume of water, the main justification for their use would be for stream and waterfall units, for raised or semi-raised pools or for small formal pools where the relative ease and speed of their installation is a major consideration. The installation of a preformed pool is covered on pages 32–3.

Flexible pool liners
In the late 1950s, sheets of polyethylene signaled the advent of the first flexible pool liners, providing a relatively easy method of waterproofing a hole in the ground. The two main problems associated with polyethylene for the water gardener were its susceptibility to hardening and cracking in areas exposed to ultraviolet light, and its ease of puncturing, with no obvious means of repair. While polyethylene continues to be used in water where it is not exposed to light, it has been superseded by the development of a new generation of polymers in the 1960s, resulting in the emergence of polyvinyl chloride (PVC) as a pool-lining material. This material not only has a much longer life than polyethylene when exposed to ultraviolet light, but it can also be easily repaired when punctured.

As PVC became more widely used, double thicknesses were welded together to give extra strength, sometimes incorporating a nylon mesh between the layers. Although originally manufactured in a wide range of colors, the shades have now become more subdued, in recognition of the fact that algae cover most of the surface under water after a few months, and that dark colors prove longer-lasting when exposed to daylight.

Shortly after the development of PVC as a pool liner, a synthetic rubber product known as Butyl rubber made its debut on the water-gardening market. It was an instant success, having all the properties required of a pool liner: flexibility, strength, durability and ease of fabrication and repair. One of its greatest assets is its resistance to deterioration in ultraviolet light, making it the best material for use in lakes, ponds and reservoirs, a fact borne out by its continued popularity with professional pool installers. PVC and Butyl rubber formulations are marketed under a variety of trade names and continue to be improved in their durability and strength. Both products are widely used and make the ideal materials for the construction of a great variety of water garden styles, although Butyl rubber, a material which stretches, tends to be more costly than its non-stretch equivalent, PVC.

Because of the limited application and the drawbacks of preformed pool liners, we concentrate on showing the stages of construction for a flexible pool liner, although several of these stages apply also to preformed pool liners.

Using flexible liners

The proposed shape for the pool should be marked out with pegs approximately 6 in. long and 1 in. square; these can also be used to indicate levels around the outline. If the pool is formal, in the shape of a rectangle or square, the corner points will need fixing first, using a simple builder's square or string (see below). Repeat the process at all four corners; then check that the lengths of the two diameter measurements across the square or rectangle are equal. Insert stout pegs to secure the strings needed for marking out the sides later. A circle is easier to mark out, using a piece of string.

Informal pools are less exacting to mark out and a garden hose or clothesline can be laid on the ground to make the shape. When a satisfactory outline is achieved, pegs should be knocked in around the perimeter and the garden hose then removed. For both formal and informal shapes, tie string between the pegs, once they are all in place, to identify the outline before digging. Or mark the outline with sand, using the pegs as a guide.

Identifying levels

Once the shape of the pool has been finalized, its proposed level will need to be fixed. On a totally level site this would be unnecessary, but most sites have a slight gradient, no matter how level they may

Fixing corner points

Construct a builder's square by joining three lengths of 2 in. × 1 in. straight-edged timber at their ends to form a triangle with the sides in the ratio of 3:4:5; minimum lengths need to be 24 in., 32 in. and 40 in. Position the shortest side on the base of the proposed outline, the right angle against the corner peg. String can be used: measure 3 ft. along the baseline from the corner and insert another peg; strike arcs with two strings, one 4 ft. from the corner peg, the other 5 ft. from the second peg.

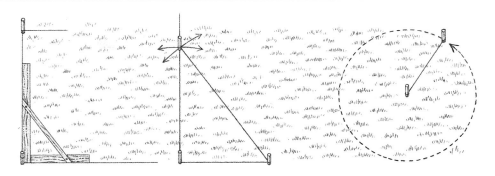

The side of the triangle projecting out from the baseline forms a right angle.

A right angle is formed between the corner peg and where the string arcs intersect.

Marking out a circle: *Fix string cut to the circle's radius to a central peg; mark around it.*

In this well-constructed pool edge, the liner has been taken under the first course of edging bricks and then brought up vertically between the first and second brick course. This allows the water level to be contained against the face of the brick edge without seeping away underneath the edging.

Excavating the site

Where the site of the pool is covered in grass, the sod should be cut into 1 ft. squares, 1–2 in. thick, and removed. Stack these squares neatly out of view, grass side down, and they will provide a valuable source of fibrous loam in a few months' time. Similarly you should find a suitable site to store the removed topsoil. Unless you are able to use the subsoil that you have excavated for contour-building around the edges of your pond, make arrangements to remove it from the site.

Once the sod has been removed, take off the topsoil to a depth of 9 in. Remove the soil at the pool sides by spade, to achieve a clean and accurate cut, even if a machine is available to excavate the central area. Dig the sides of the hole at a very slight angle from the vertical—preferably no more than 20 degrees, which is 1 in. from the vertical for every 3 in. of depth. If the excavated soil needs to be temporarily stored on an adjacent area of lawn, protect the grass with a plastic sheet before heaping up the mound of soil.

look to the naked eye. Taking care to ensure that the pool has a level surround prevents exposure of the liner, which would spoil the pool's appearance.

If the site has a gradient, in order to achieve the proposed water level it will be necessary either to build up the edge on the lower side or to cut away the ground on the higher level. If the ground climbs up from the house, it is better to cut away at the higher point. Conversely, if the ground slopes away from the house, you should build up the land at the lower end of the pool. Use ample soil or other material such as sand and consolidate it well to prevent later movement through water pressure inside the liner.

Marginal shelves

Having removed the topsoil, you need to determine and mark the position of the marginal shelves, using a thin scattering of sand as a guideline. These will allow shallow-water plants to be accommodated later

Establishing relative levels

Make a line on one of the marking pegs to act as a reference peg or datum point. You will need to make any height adjustments to the other pegs by spanning a straight-edged length of timber with a level on the top from one peg to another, around the pool. The pool should now have a clearly defined boundary, with pegs indicating a level pool edge. If the soil is very sandy, it is a useful precaution to knock in the pegs a little outside the pool boundary in case they become dislodged when digging out starts.

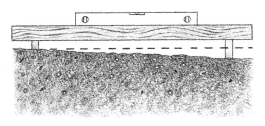

The undulations of a site can be deceptive: the only way to identify level changes across the site with any certainty is to use a level and a long board.

Adjust the height of the pegs so that they are all level, right around the pool.

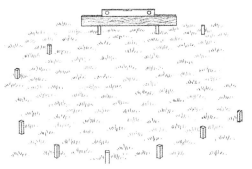

in planting crates or as permanent planting. In formal pools, marginal shelves may surround the pool completely, as there is generally no area at the side of the pool in which to grow bog or moisture-loving plants. The shelves are 9 in. deep and generally 10–12 in. wide; if you wish to accommodate permanent marginal planting beds, the shelves will need to be wider (see page 46). The marginal shelves must remain undisturbed during the process of excavation to give better stability to the sides of the deeper zone.

The deeper zone

The central, or deep, zone can now be dug out, keeping the subsoil separate from any topsoil already removed. This deeper zone should be excavated to a final depth of 1½–2 ft., but in areas prone to severe winters, or in very large ponds, this depth can be increased to 2½ ft. The sides of the deeper zone should be cut out at a slight angle from the vertical as before.

Preparing for the liner

If there is a local supplier, you should obtain the liner after the excavation is complete, to ensure that it matches the hole accurately. Although a liner is normally ordered and delivered before work starts,

adjustments are sometimes made during the excavation process, either because of unforeseen problems or through modifications in the shape of the pool as work proceeds, so if you can delay ordering the liner until after excavating, this is a good precaution.

Calculating the liner size

Liners can be ordered to most rectangular sizes by mail order or in certain roll widths when collected at an aquatic center. It is not necessary to allow extra for the small surplus flap of liner around the edges where high-quality stretch materials like Butyl rubber are used and where the side walls have been cut out at a slight angle. With non-stretch materials like polyethylene and some of the cheaper PVC liners, it is worth adding an extra 1 ft. to both length and width. This applies also to the liners for raised pools. If you are intending to make an adjacent bog area at the same time as the pool itself, you will need to take this into account when making your calculations for the liner (see page 58).

Protecting the liner

Before placing a liner into a freshly dug hole, rake over the surface and remove any stones or materials with sharp edges which could puncture the liner. Take time to examine the sides and bottom carefully and once you are satisfied that no sharp edges remain, drape a cushioning blanket of polyester matting or

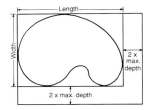

MEASURING FOR THE LINER
In order to calculate the size of liner required, measure the depth of the pool and double it. Add this figure to the pool's maximum length for the length of liner needed, and add this same figure to the pool's maximum width to work out the width required.

Digging out for the pool

Having fixed the outline and proposed level of the pool, with pegs positioned just outside the proposed perimeter, remove the topsoil to a depth of 9 in. Dig the edge of the pool outline slightly sloping, to give extra rigidity to the sides. Mark the inside of the marginal-shelf outline 9–12 in. inside the pool perimeter, then dig out the deeper zone with slightly sloping sides. Check the final level of the pool floor by measuring down from a straight plank of wood that straddles the sides of the pool.

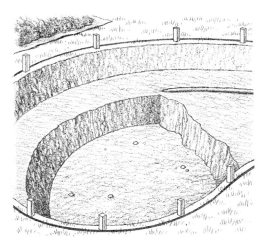

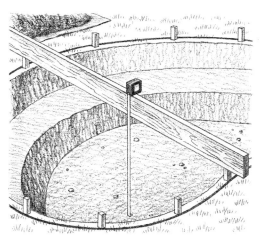

padding (available from good aquatic centers) into the excavation as insurance against any sharp surface. This is needed particularly on stony ground or land which has previously been a landfill site and contains rubble. This matting also provides permanent protection, unlike damp newspaper, which is sometimes recommended as a lining material. A lining of moist sand may also be used to cushion the liner, but as it can easily be dislodged from the side walls when the main liner is installed, the walls of the pool could be left unprotected.

Installing the liner

Because large PVC and Butyl rubber liners are quite heavy, it is useful to find out from the supplier how the liner has been folded in order to avoid unnecessary dragging or lifting, which may disturb the underlay when unfolding. Try to enlist as much help as possible in order to hold each corner in place before draping the liner into the excavation. Unfold a smaller liner on any adjacent lawn first and, if the weather is sunny, leave it for a while to warm up and become more flexible before fitting it into the excavated hole, as shown in the illustration below.

The appearance of folds and wrinkles is inevitable when you are fitting a rectangular liner into box-like holes, and although conspicuous at first in the clear, fresh water, the folds soon become less apparent under water pressure and the eventual covering of

algae. Liners for circular pools or more complex shapes can be prefabricated by some suppliers to fit the excavation exactly, eliminating any folds.

As the water nears its finished level, any minor adjustments to low edges can be made by adding sand or soil behind the liner. Do not cut off any surplus liner until you are sure that no leaks or low points occur and the water is held at the desired level for a day or two. You can now finish the edges by one of the methods described on pages 40–4.

Cobblestones have been used as part of the edging for this pool, discreetly covering the flexible liner. In addition to their aesthetic appeal, cobblestones make an excellent material for shallow-sided ponds, and a pleasant contrast to dense planting.

Fitting the liner into the hole

If using a Butyl rubber liner, there is no need to push the liner into every corner of the excavation, since the weight of the water and the stretch property of the Butyl rubber will allow it to settle naturally into the contours. Drape the liner evenly over the excavation and secure it with stones at the sides which would otherwise be pulled inward as the liner settles down. If using a cheaper liner, take care to insert it evenly across the bottom and place stones or bricks on the overlap around the edges to secure it against wind.

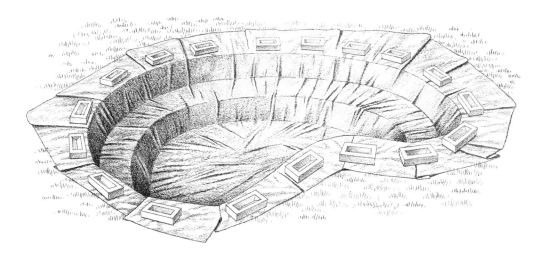

Fitting preformed pools

Once the shape of the pool has been marked out (see below), and the pool mold removed, the bamboo canes can be replaced by shorter pegs or an outline of sand. Then the pool outline is checked for levels in the same way as described for flexible liners (see page 29). You are then ready to start digging out the hole. Starting from 4 in. outside the pool's outline, remove the topsoil to a depth of 9 in., cutting the sides of the hole at a slightly sloping angle from the vertical. If the pool has marginal shelves and an evenly shaped, flat-bottomed base, lift the pool back carefully into the hole so that the base will easily make an impression on the soft soil, particularly if it has been raked beforehand. The impression indicates the area of soil which will have to be dug out to accommodate the full depth of the pool. Dig this inner hole 3 in. deeper than the depth of the pool liner itself, to allow for a foundation of sand, and 4 in. wider to allow for the sloping sides.

If the mold has no appreciable area of flat base and contains numerous marginal shelves at various depths, it is better to take out the whole excavation to the full depth of the pool, adding the extra depth of 3 in. for the foundation and 4 in. all around the sides. It is very difficult to make an impression of the mold's base for this type of complex pool profile.

Line the base of the excavation with 3 in. of sand and insert the pool liner gently into the hole, temporarily stabilizing it by bricks if it is unsteady. Make a check across the top edges of the pool in several directions to ensure that it is sitting level, by using a level on top of a straight-edged piece of timber long enough to span the pool. Any necessary alteration is then made in the soft sand foundation beneath the pool to create a completely level surround. You can then start filling the pool up with water, and backfilling with sand or soil to fill in the spaces in the excavation, as shown below. Make regular checks on the levels as the work proceeds.

Once the pool is installed, the surround may need disguising (see page 33). Where a preformed pool is used to make a raised pool, it can be either partially buried in the soil or be freestanding on the surface.

Raised pools

A raised pool can be made using either a preformed liner or a flexible liner, and all raised pools need to have a surround to disguise the sides. As the pre-fabricated pool is a solid waterproof structure and would not exert any water pressure outside the mold, the raised surround, made of brick, timber, stone or rocks, need only be strong enough to contain any soil or sand which is backfilled behind the surround for the pool's stability. But for raised pools using a flexible liner, twin walls with a cavity between them

Marking out the shape

If the preformed pool is a symmetrical shape, such as a square or rectangle, it can be laid upside down on the proposed site to mark its outline with sand or pegs prior to the excavation. As an irregular, informal shape would be the wrong way around when the pool is inverted, it needs to be stood upright in the desired position and temporarily stabilized with boxes or bricks while you indicate its outline with bamboo canes, forming vertical markers between the edge of the surround and ground level.

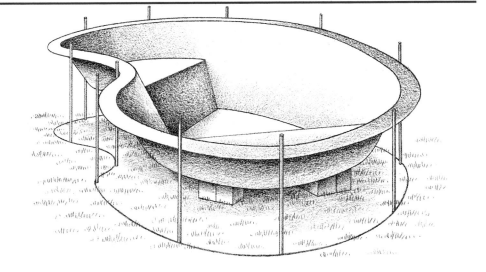

Dark-colored bricks have been used to construct the surrounding walls of this split-level raised pool, with light-colored paving used as a coping. Attention to detail in creating a dead-level surround is important when using a light-colored coping, as the stones' reflections are particularly dominant against the dark sides of the pool. If the pool is high enough the coping makes an ideal casual seat, provided the stones are between 9 and 12 in. in width.

are needed to provide greater strength against internal water pressure and better insulation against the exposure to cold above ground level; the methods of inserting the liner are shown on page 34.

Making a surround

Bricks and stone blocks are both excellent materials for surrounding raised pools, particularly in a formal garden. Once the outline of a raised pool has been marked out as described on page 32, a small trench needs to be dug along the pool outline to allow a concrete foundation to be laid for the side walls of the pool. If the soil is very light, a 3–4 in. layer of gravel should first be consolidated at the bottom of the trench to give extra reinforcement. A suitable mix for the foundation would be one part cement, three parts sharp sand and six parts aggregate. When winter temperatures drop below 20°F, follow local masonry practice regarding foundation, mix ratio and reinforcements. Protect the drying concrete from extremes of heat and cold by using wet sacking in hot weather or polyethylene in frosty weather.

After two or three days the foundations will have set and be strong enough to bear the weight of the pool walls. Unless you are experienced in bricklaying it is advisable to employ the skills of a professional to build the walls. But before these are built you will need to consider the alternative methods of incorporating the liner (see below) and decide which to use.

Putting the pool in place

Once the surround is level, add 4 in. of water to the pool to create extra stability and then backfill loosely with sand or soil to the same depth around the outside of the mold. Firm this backfilling in place by tamping the soil with a thick stick as the work proceeds. Once the first 4 in. layer of soil is backfilled and the surround checked for level again, add another 4 in. of water to the pool before backfilling with more soil or sand outside. Keep repeating this process until the pool mold is completely installed.

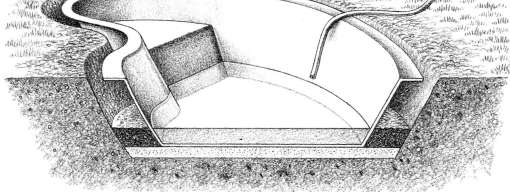

Fitting the liner

The first method involves draping the liner inside the inner wall and feeding it into the cavity below the top two brick courses of the inner wall. The overlapping flap of liner is then laid under the coping stone and sandwiched in the mortar, securing it to the twin walls. Feeding the liner below the top two courses prevents white marks and provides a more attractive finish. With the bulk of the liner on the inside of the inner wall, cavity wall ties can be placed in the soft mortar between the bricks below the top two courses, strengthening the walls. This also allows a cheaper material to be used for the inside wall below the top two courses, as it will be hidden.

The second method involves draping the liner completely inside the cavity from the pool bottom to the coping. The liner has to be placed in position before the inner wall is built and is then totally hidden. It is the more expensive method because it requires top-quality bricks or stone to be used for both walls. It also prevents cavity wall ties from being used. As with the first method, the weight of the coping stones is adequate to bed the surplus flap of liner onto the mortar at the top of the walls.

Prior to draping the liner inside a raised or semi-raised pool by whichever method, the liner should be protected against sharp edges by placing a layer of polyester matting or padding underneath. This is particularly important when the liner covers a marginal shelf constructed of bricks or blocks (see page 35). After lining the whole excavated area with protective matting, drape the waterproof membrane evenly in the raised pool, ensuring that any overlap is equal on opposite sides. Where the inner wall is to be built on top of the liner and the liner sandwiched between the two walls, stretch the bottom of the liner and hide any folds before the walls are built.

When measuring for liners of raised pools, allow an extra 1 ft. in both length and width for the flap for mortaring under the coping, as their vertical side walls, unlike sloping sides, leave no margin for any surplus on installation (see page 30).

Coping stones

The choice of coping should complement the color of the brick or stone used in the wall or any surrounding paving. If it is possible to use the same paving slabs, this ties the feature more strongly into the overall design of the pool. The height of the walls and the width of the coping stones are especially important if the walls of the pool are to be used as seating. To be comfortable, the walls need to be a minimum of 2 ft. above ground level and the coping a minimum width of 1 ft. The coping stones should overlap the inside edge of the wall by about 2–2¾ in. over the water to produce interesting shadows and to hide the mortar. It is useful when mortaring

This formal raised pool has been extended to create an independent bog garden which is separated from the main pool area by a brick wall. By using the same brick edging around the small bog garden the two features are nicely tied together, particularly when the glorious blue leaves of Hosta sieboldiana *overlap the pool and pick out the hue of the bricks. The water lily leaves are complemented by the rosettes of water lettuce (*Pistia stratiotes*) floating on the surface of the pool.*

Digging the trench for the foundations

Dig a trench 1½ ft. wide and 10–12 in. deep; then drive in pegs along the center line. Level their tops by using a level on top of a straight-edged piece of timber that spans the distance from one peg to another. The peg tops will indicate the level to which the wet concrete has to be poured. After watering the trench and any gravel thoroughly, to prevent the fresh concrete from drying out too rapidly and cracking, pour in the concrete mix. Tamp it down and level it to the tops of the pegs.

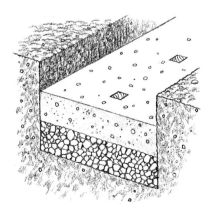

Incorporating the liner in the wall

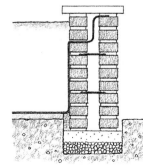
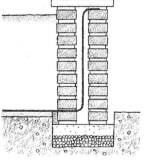

Liner inside the inner wall   *Liner inside the cavity*

the coping in place to incorporate a length of conduit, which allows easier threading of electric cable if it is needed later for a submersible pump (see page 47) or lighting.

Marginal shelves for raised pools

As with a sunken pool, an area of shallow water around the edge of a raised pool allows a greater variety of plants to be grown in the water. Where the flexible liner has been incorporated behind the top

two brick courses of the inner wall, the marginal shelf needs to be built before the liner is inserted, using prefabricated blocks or subsoil. Where the liner is totally sandwiched between the pool walls, a better-quality brick or stone can be mortared into place on top of the liner. If you need to stand inside the pool while working, protect the liner from damage and mortar by sheets of cardboard or polyethylene.

Semi-raised pools

A pool which is partially raised makes a good compromise for certain situations and its construction saves considerably on the materials required to build a totally raised pool. For a semi-raised pool with a 1 ft. high surround, the outline is marked out as on page 30 and the foundations prepared for the low surround as shown below, left. The excavation for the deeper water area is then made 1 ft. inside the foundations to a depth of 1 ft. The original ground level then acts as the marginal shelf. Other methods of inserting the liner described above need to be considered before building the low surround walls.

Semi-raised pools with surrounds no higher than 1–1½ ft. make excellent fountain pools. If a heavy central fountain is to be installed, there is no need to make a deeper central excavation, because a large concrete slab or a specially built foundation will need to be supported by undisturbed soil.

Making marginal shelves

Where the liner is to be incorporated behind the top two brick courses of the inner wall, place walling blocks 9 in. wide on top of each other to within 9 in. of the top of the wall. As they will be under the liner and held in place by water pressure they do not need mortaring. Where a sandwiched liner is used, the walls of marginal shelves are built onto the liner, using surplus liner on top of the original liner as protection. Mortar blocks into place to create a shelf 9 in. wide and 9 in. below the water line.

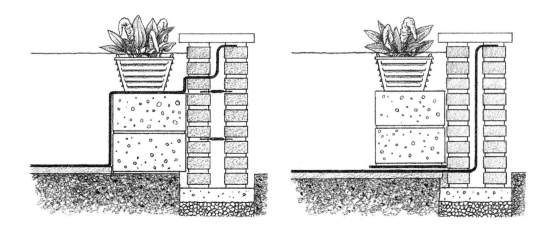

Making a wildlife pool

Where there is a very heavy clay soil and a tendency for water to accumulate in a depression, boggy wildlife pools can often be created without having to use a liner. Water retention is increased if the depression in the land is consolidated after bailing out or pumping out any existing water. On a large scale, this is done by running heavy mechanical equipment or rollers repeatedly over the depression. On a small scale, repeated pummeling with a 7 lb. hammer or wooden rammers will consolidate the soil sufficiently to make the clay less impervious. An alternative is to import clay during the summer and line the depression with a 4–5 in. layer of clay lumps, which are then spread and consolidated.

If the existing soil is not appropriate for consolidating, and it is not convenient to import clay, a liner will need to be installed and then covered with a layer of soil 6 in. thick to allow the plants to root freely and grow without too much restriction. Some restraint is necessary to prevent vigorous marginal plants such as bulrushes from totally overrunning the water surface, however, and this can be achieved by ensuring that there is an adequate area of deeper water (about 2 ft.) in the middle of the pool, where the marginals will not survive.

Beds can be created to contain the vigorous mar-ginal aquatics by digging out bowl-shaped holes of various depths and sizes adjacent to the pool before placing a liner over the whole area and backfilling with soil. As long as the dividing walls between the holes are just below the water level of the pool, water will be able to seep from the pool into the beds to enable the marginals to grow satisfactorily. The pool only needs to have a covering of 6 in. of soil before filling it up with water, but all the surrounding bowl-shaped areas will be completely filled with soil to just above the water level in the main pool. No liner is then seen in the bog garden area around the pool, but the plants are contained.

An alternative method of containing vigorous plants is to build a submerged retaining wall onto the pool liner to separate soil and water. In an oval or elliptically shaped outline, the wall is ideally con-structed across the width of the pool, leaving approximately two-thirds of the pool with deeper water. The top of the wall should finish approxi-mately 4–6 in. below the water surface, and should be constructed with waterproof colored bricks. The wall is mortared onto the liner using any spare offcuts on top of the liner as extra protection. Allow the cement to dry out for a day or two, then fill the planting area with soil to the top of the wall.

Constructing a wildlife pool

Mark out the pool's outline with a garden hose or clothesline; then follow the stages of construction for a flexible liner (see page 28), with one major difference. As the perimeter of a wildlife pool requires an area devoted to a shallow beach, this area must be given a gentle gradient of about 30 degrees in the excavation. Insert the liner as described on page 31 and spread a 6 in. layer of soil over the flat surfaces. Hide the edge of the liner above the marginal shelves by folding the liner into the surrounding soil.

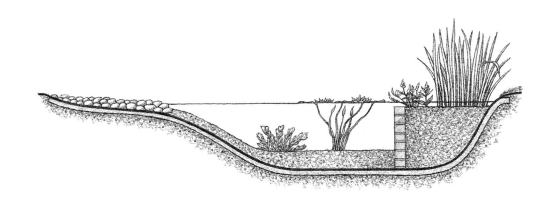

This wildlife pool is situated near woodland, where it is able to attract animals and birds that will visit the pool regularly to drink along the shallow sides. A variety of wild plants, including blue-flowered echium, attracts a greater variety of insects to the poolside, where they will act as pollinators and be a valuable food supply to amphibians.

Acorus calamus

The generic name of this plant derives from the Greek akoron, *meaning a plant with aromatic roots. The rhizomes of sweet flag have been used extensively in perfumery and to provide a bitter tang in alcoholic drinks; sections of root about 4 in. long are dried until brittle. Like many rushes, the sword-like leaves were used as a floor covering in dwellings and churches in medieval Britain.*

A wildlife pool with a bog area

This wildlife pool, measuring 13 × 8 ft., is shown in spring. It consists largely of a bog area separated from the deeper water by a submerged retaining wall, containing tall marginals such as flag iris *(Iris pseudacorus)*, with spiky leaves and yellow flowers, and a variegated grass, *Glyceria maxima* var. *variegata*, whose cream-striped leaves are edged with a delicate pink. Vigorous moisture-loving plants, such as deep pink loosestrife *(Lythrum salicaria)* and white-flowered *Senecio smithii*, border this area and extend the interest into the autumn. A small cobble-stone beach enables amphibians to move in and out of the pool and to hide under the floating leaves of water fringe *(Nymphoides peltata)* and fairy moss *(Azolla caroliniana)*. The main pool's margins are interspersed with clumps of pendulous sedge *(Carex pendula)*, whose long, graceful flowers extend over the water, and the intriguing flowers of cotton grass *(Eriophorum angustifolium)* alongside the beach.

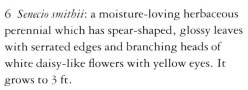

1 *Calla palustris*: a shallow-water marginal for the poolside with creeping surface rhizomes supporting shiny, firm, heart-shaped leaves and arum-like white flowers. It grows to 1 ft.

2 *Polygonum bistorta*: a moisture-loving, herbaceous perennial with broad pokers of pink flowers during summer above strong, ovate leaves. It grows to 2½ ft.

3 *Veronica beccabunga*: a shallow-water marginal with creeping, succulent, almost evergreen stems and small blue, white-centered flowers in spring and summer. It grows to 4 in.

4 *Iris pseudacorus*: a vigorous marginal aquatic with tall spiky leaves and yellow flowers in spring. It grows to 4 ft.

5 *Butomus umbellatus*: a shallow-water marginal with tall, thin rush-like leaves and umbels of pink flowers, held above the leaves, which have conspicuous red stamens from mid- to late summer. This marginal plant grows to 3 ft.

6 *Senecio smithii*: a moisture-loving herbaceous perennial which has spear-shaped, glossy leaves with serrated edges and branching heads of white daisy-like flowers with yellow eyes. It grows to 3 ft.

7 *Lythrum salicaria*: a moisture-loving herbaceous perennial with spikes of bright magenta flowers in late summer above bushy clumps of lance-shaped leaves. It grows to 5 ft.

8 *Filipendula ulmaria*: a moisture-loving herbaceous perennial with creamy-white, feathery spikes above deeply cut leaves in mid-summer. It grows to 3–5 ft.

9 *Glyceria maxima* var. *variegata*: a vigorous marginal plant with striking, grass-like leaves, striped with green, white and cream. Straw-colored panicles are produced from mid- to late summer. It grows to 3 ft.

10 *Sagittaria sagittifolia*: a spreading marginal plant with fine, shiny, arrow-shaped leaves and spikes of white-petaled flowers from mid- to late summer. It grows to 1½ ft.

11 *Ranunculus flammula*: a marginal aquatic producing numerous small, golden-yellow flowers on reddish stems with dark green oval leaves. It grows to 1½ ft.

12 *Mentha aquatica*: a spreading aquatic with whorls of axillary, lilac flowers in mid- to late summer, at the base of the strong-smelling mint leaves. It grows to 3 ft.

13 *Aruncus dioicus*: a moisture-loving herbaceous perennial with tall spikes of feathery white flowers in late summer which are held above deeply cut leaves. It grows to 5 ft.

14 *Cardamine pratensis*: a moisture-lover producing tufts of cress-like leaves and small spikes of rosy-lilac flowers in late spring. It grows to 1½ ft.

15 *Caltha palustris*: a marginal aquatic which produces waxy, yellow, buttercup-like flowers in early spring from a clump of dark green, almost circular leaves. It grows to 1½ ft.

16 *Alisma plantago-aquatica*: a marginal aquatic producing a rosette of long-stalked, ovate leaves and spikes of rosy-white flowers in mid-summer. The old flower spikes remain attractive throughout autumn and early winter.

It grows to 2½ ft.

17 *Acorus calamus* 'Variegatus': a vigorous marginal aquatic with sword-like, cream-variegated leaves and inconspicuous flowers. It grows to 3 ft.

18 *Eriophorum angustifolium*: a spreading marginal aquatic with coarse foliage and tassles of white, cotton-wool-like flowers in mid- to late summer. It grows to 1 ft.

19 *Carex pendula*: a vigorous shallow-water marginal aquatic with slender grass-like leaves and long, drooping, elegant flower spikes. It grows to 3 ft.

20 *Nymphoides peltata*: a submerged aquatic which has floating, mottled, heart-shaped leaves and small yellow flowers with fringed edges, produced in mid- to late summer. Water depth: 4–30 in.

21 *Azolla caroliniana*: a floating aquatic whose carpets of small, tightly packed, fern-like plants, with delicate, pale green leaves, turn red in the autumn.

22 *Stratiotes aloides* (water soldier): a submerged aquatic whose spiky leaves appear partially above the water. Water depth: 1½–2 ft.

Edging formal pools

The choice of edging is a major decision in the design of a formal pool and a successful choice will complement the pool's reflections, particularly of any marginal planting. Attention to detail is especially important in the edging of formal pools. Any slight variation in level will be conspicuous when adjacent to an unbroken water surface and will be exaggerated when reflected in the water. Safety is paramount and a firm, non-slip surface must be a priority if the pool sides are used as a main pathway or viewing area.

Formal pools are normally edged with paving slabs, bricks or timber. Where the pool is surrounded by paving, the slabs are taken right up to the pool edge to create a slight overlap of 2 in. over the water. Alternatively, by using bricks set at right angles to the water's edge, the pool surround creates a complete contrast to the rest of the paving. The particular advantages and disadvantages of alternative materials are outlined below. A pool which has the water level at the same height as the top of the surrounding paving is known as a brimming pool. Such a pool makes a particularly effective reflective surface, to frame an architectural feature or a group of plants. Bricks make the most suitable edging material, needing less liner to be extended underneath than large stone slabs.

Natural stone Large slabs of natural stone paving look effective in settings where natural stone predominates. Reclaimed stone paving, with its weathered, riven surface, makes an appropriate paving edge to pools near older property. Reclaimed stone comes in a variety of sizes and thicknesses, and the pieces to be used around formal water need careful selection to achieve a uniform thickness parallel with the water surface. The larger slabs allow a good width of overlap to the water and give excellent stability when mortared over the edge. The main disadvantage of much reclaimed stone paving is that its surface is slippery when wet. Algae grow on natural stone more readily than on man-made materials and become lethal if allowed to grow unchecked near the water's edge. Frequent scrubbing with algicide will prevent their taking hold—follow instructions and take care not to spill any chemical into the pool.

Reconstructed stone or concrete paving slabs Reconstituted rectangular stone slabs make an excellent pool edge and are less slippery than the natural material, particularly the types which have textured or anti-slip surfaces. Although manufactured in a wide variety of sizes and shades to blend or contrast

Paving around the pool

Prepare the area for paving the pool surround by removing the soil to pool level. If the soil is light and sandy, remove a further 2–4 in. and replace this with consolidated gravel to provide a firmer base. Lay any overlap of flexible liner on the soil surface or the gravel and place dabs of freshly mixed mortar around the pool edge, sealing the liner to the ground. Lay dabs of mortar under the corners and center of each paving stone too; the mortar mix should consist of one part cement to four parts sand.

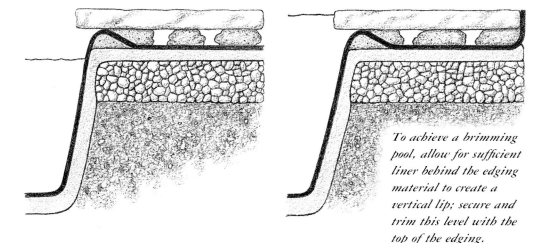

To achieve a brimming pool, allow for sufficient liner behind the edging material to create a vertical lip; secure and trim this level with the top of the edging.

Bricks Bricks make a sophisticated edge to formal pools, particularly when a contrasting color is used to the surrounding paving. Although there is insufficient length bricks to create an overlap to the water, their size and shape make them ideal for both regular and curving outlines.

Timber Wood makes a good association with water, especially in the form of decking, which can overlap the water much farther than other edging material and completely disguise unsightly edges like those of fiberglass liners. Flexible liners can be stapled to the underside of decking above the water line, making it very suitable for long, straight edges. Old railroad ties provide a stable and successful method of edging a partially raised pool.

Use any timber preservative carefully near water since most preservatives are harmful to fish and plant life. For the same reason, freshly painted timber should not be used if it would be in contact with water. Certain timbers are pressure-treated at the sawmills to resist rot, and advice should be sought from the lumber merchant to check for any possible harmful effects on plant life and fish. Softwoods such as pine are notoriously resinous and the resin can prove toxic to submerged plant and animal life.

when laid together, they have the advantage of being a standard thickness, which is valuable at the water's edge, where parallel levels are important. Use the largest size of slab to form a pool surround; this will not only provide an attractive overlap to the water but will also give sufficient stability.

Random paving Irregular paving is useful for providing an edge to irregular or circular outlines. Unfortunately it is often used as a total surround for informal ponds, which prevents any area of the water's edge being planted with bog or moisture-loving plants. It can be extremely variable in thickness and size. When ordering irregular paving, insist on large pieces with a uniform thickness; if possible, check the material before it is delivered.

Edging informal pools

Whereas formal pool edges are often rigid and straight, allowing the same material to be used all around the pond, the edging of informal water enables a greater variety of materials to create a gradual and more natural transition from water to land. Liners should be invisible above the water line and there are various methods of achieving this.

Using rocks

Rocks make an ideal edging for informal water, particularly when the gaps between partially submerged rocks create wet pockets of soil in which to grow marginal plants. The more impermeable the rock, the less likely it is to shatter from the effects of severe frost. Very soft sandstones absorb a considerable volume of water and in milder districts provide excellent moist surfaces for the colonization of mosses and ferns. When a large number of these rocks are used to landscape the sides of pools and streams, the disadvantage of their absorbent nature is the volume of water evaporating from the moist rocks in hot weather. This evaporation increases the need for frequent topping off with tap water which encourages the submerged green algae that feed on the mineral salts in the tap water. Granite and slate,

unlike sandstone, do not absorb water and are particularly useful for streams or dramatic rocky landscaping where waterfalls are included. Their hard consistency resists frost damage and their surfaces are less sympathetic to the development of moss or algae than softer rocks.

Weatherworn limestone must be used with caution as it is alkaline and could have an adverse effect on the water chemistry. Being light in color when freshly quarried, it is particularly conspicuous in a non-limestone area. Good weatherworn samples are increasingly costly because of declining resources, and the stones, with their deep and interesting fissures, would be wasted if partly submerged.

Locally quarried stone is normally the answer, both in suitability and value for money. When used solely to edge a pool, there is little justification in importing costly stone. Where the rock will form part of a surrounding landscape feature, however, its impact may justify the extra expense in specifying rocks from farther afield and the type, size and shape of the pieces delivered. Try to visit the supplier or quarry beforehand to assess the available stone and to discuss the size and quantity required. Try to avoid giving the appearance of a wall by having too many rocks of the same size and thickness.

Caltha palustris
From early-spring until early-summer, marsh marigolds grace wetlands in temperate climates with cheerful masses of waxy yellow flowers, particularly in partial shade. The other common name of kingcup is derived from the old English "cop," meaning a button or stud in a style such as kings once wore. Such tight buds were also pickled like capers. It was a custom on May Day for farmers to hang marsh marigolds over cattle sheds to protect them from the evil-doings of fairies and witches.

Positioning rocks

As the rocks will sit on the liner, they should be bedded onto a stiff mix of mortar to minimize any risk of damage and to make the rocks stable. Select pieces approximately the same thickness as the depth of the marginal shelf. Position the rocks on the inside edge of the shelf, flattest side downward, allowing space behind the rocks for planting. The tops of the rocks can vary in height to look natural. Ensure that the edge of the liner is well above the water line behind the rocks before it is covered with soil.

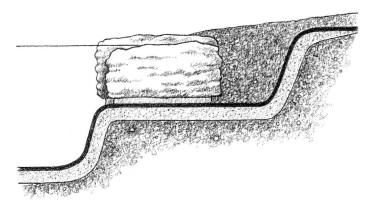

Rocks make a useful and appropriate edging material for informal pools, particularly when they are used to make a division between water and wet soil where marginal plants can be grown. Ideally a local, non-porous stone should be used. Water forget-me-not (Myosotis scorpioides) and the variegated dwarf sedge (Acorus gramineus 'Variegatus') help to soften the rocks, which contain the rampant roots of the tall reedmace (Typha latifolia).

As an edging to water, rocks look better when partially submerged. The marginal shelf made in the initial construction (see page 35) makes an ideal platform on which to place rocks, but if it is only 9 in. deep and 1 ft. wide, it may be too deep or too narrow to accommodate the size of rock chosen. Where the rocks are to form a large proportion of the pool edge, it is a great advantage to have the rock on site before building the pool. The marginal shelf can then be constructed to suit the rocks and still allow ample room for marginal planting in the wet soil behind them.

In some cases, large pieces of flattish-shaped rocks can be used around the pool just above the water line in the same way as paving stones edge a formal pool (see page 40). In this situation the edge of the liner is laid flat just under or just behind the rock. The positioning of these more exposed rocks is crucial. In order to achieve a coordinated but natural appearance, they should have their flattest side uppermost and nearly level with the top side of any other rocks parallel to the first stone installed. If their top sides tilt in different directions this will have a restless effect on the pool's tranquillity. These exposed rocks should be bedded onto mortar, as below.

Cobblestone surrounds

Cobblestones make good pool edges, particularly where the pool is constructed with a shallow gradient, enabling the cobblestones to be seen both above and below the water line. A rise or fall in the water level is less obvious on the shallow gradient of the pool sides than it is on vertical or steep faces. Cobblestone edges are popular as beaches in wildlife pools, and to add interest the stones should be mixed in size and have variation in the width of cover, preventing a monotonous or artificial ribbon-like surround where they form the majority of the water's edge.

A pool with a shallow gradient forming the complete edge needs to be extensive in size in order to contain a sufficient ratio of water depth to water surface. In a small pond with shallow, saucer-like edges all the way around there is a greater tendency for algae and blanketweed to build up in the warm, shallow water, so it is better for small ponds to keep this style of edge to a minimum. The gradient should be sufficiently shallow for the cobblestones to look stable enough not to roll down into the water. To improve stability, the cobblestones can be bedded in concrete, but it has to be said that freely placed cobblestones look more natural.

Cobblestones can be obtained in several colors and locally obtained material looks more natural than those imported from a different ecological area. White cobblestones are striking in their impact but must be used with caution in an informal pool. Place some larger specimen cobblestones among the smaller sizes to add interest and give a more random appearance. Be generous in their placing: if sparsely used, the liner can be seen and the effect will be spoiled. In fact, coarse sand used between the cobblestones looks better than bare liner.

As the cover could extend beyond the edge of the liner, gradually introduce planting among the cobblestones so that the transition to a thicker planting of grass looks less artificial. Many aquatic plants look particularly effective emerging from between cobblestones in the very shallow water.

Lawn edging

Forming the edge of a pool with a gently sloping lawn is both effective and natural-looking. From a practical point of view, you will need to create a definite edge between grass and water to prevent the grass edge crumbling into the water, particularly if it is subject to heavy wear. This can be achieved by creating a strong vertical support at the water's edge using stone or short timber poles; this prevents any subsiding of the grass and creates a clearly defined edge which can be trimmed easily. Once you have made the supporting edge, sod can be laid on the backfilled layer of soil, the edge of the sod finishing at the top of the poles, or the inside edge of the stones. The two alternative methods of creating a supporting edge, using timber poles and using stone blocks, are illustrated below.

If you are using timber supports, the short poles look better when positioned vertically alongside each other, butting each other as closely as possible; they should be of a similar diameter, which can range between 3 and 6 in. After installing the poles, cut off their tops to a uniform height, which should be just below the level of the grass. The poles need to be no longer than 1½–2 ft. prior to trimming them. You should buy pressure-treated timber, which is safe and will resist rot, and avoid highly resinous species such as pine.

Natural walling stone or granite paving blocks can be used in the same way as poles for underpinning a lawn edge. As algae soon grow on natural stone, this should be used in preference to reconstituted stone for a more natural finish. Where a marginal shelf has been included in the design of the pool profile, this will need extending in width by 6 in. to allow a small stone wall to be built onto the liner at the outer edge of the shelf. A layer of soil should be spread over the stones before laying the sod on top.

Planted surrounds

Where plants for a normal moist or dry soil are required instead of grass at the pool edge, the device of timber poles, walling stone or rock to hide the liner can still be used to create the boundary between water and the drier soil beyond the liner. Although roots from surrounding plantings will gradually branch out to the adjacent soil, the soil in contact with the water would simply erode without some form of supporting barrier. Large fish can also cause disturbance to soil and planting at the water's edge by foraging. The leaves of plants and a thin covering of soil will soon screen the top of any edging material which looks too artificial. The planting outside the liner will not have any of the moisture from the pool, while the selection of plants at the pool side requires special beds to be constructed which are described in detail on page 46.

A cobblestone fountain makes a lively and attractive feature in all sizes of garden. For a relatively low expenditure it brings movement and noise to formal or informal areas alike by recirculating water in a small jet above a cluster of cobblestones suspended over a small reservoir by a grid. The markings on cobblestones look particularly attractive when wet and, provided the reservoir is topped up regularly in hot, dry weather, the feature requires very little maintenance.

Supporting lawn edging

Dig a small trench and line it so that the poles can be inserted on top of the liner. Fill it with wet concrete, insert poles and backfill with soil to the height of the proposed grass. Bring the edge of the liner up behind the concrete and soil to above the water line. When the cement has hardened, after two to three days, cut off the tops of the poles evenly.

Stones should be embedded into mortar on top of the liner to give stability. The liner will finish above the water line, behind the stones and just below the level of the grass.

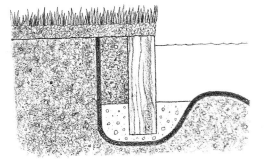

The liner finishes behind the line of poles, separated by the concrete and soil.

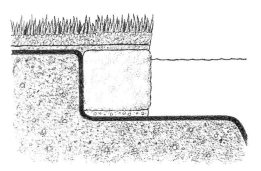

Spread a thin layer of soil on top of the stone, then lay sod over it.

Cobblestone fountains

For a cobblestone fountain covering an area 3 ft. square, a waterproof plastic trash can sunk below ground level makes the ideal reservoir. Larger jets of water and cobblestone areas will need a small sunken pool, lined with a flexible liner (see page 30), to act as the hidden reservoir.

Once you have buried the trash can in the ground, you need to install the pump, as shown below. Then connect a length of hose or rigid pipe, long enough to reach a few inches above ground level, to the outlet pipe. This will enable the height of the fountain to be regulated. Place a supporting metal grid or stout mesh across the top of the container and feed the flexible hose or rigid pipe through this grid, then position washed cobblestones on top of the grid to lodge the pipe in an upright position. Place more cobblestones over the collar of polyethylene surrounding the top of the container. When the container is filled with water and the pump turned on, the water splashes onto the cobblestones and returns to the reservoir beneath.

In periods of hot, dry weather, there will be considerable evaporation from the wet cobblestones, so the reservoir should be topped off frequently. Considerable damage will be done to the pump if it is kept running without water.

Making a cobblestone fountain using a trash can

Insert the trash can into the ground so that the rim is just below soil level. Drape a sloping, saucer-shaped collar of polyethylene or waterproof membrane from just inside the rim of the trash can to about 1½ ft. beyond the rim, to catch any water. Place a submersible pump (see page 48) inside the container, resting on a shallow base, to prevent the pump intake from silting up. Connect a flexible hose or a rigid pipe to the pump's outlet pipe. Place a grid on top of the container; then cover it with cobblestones.

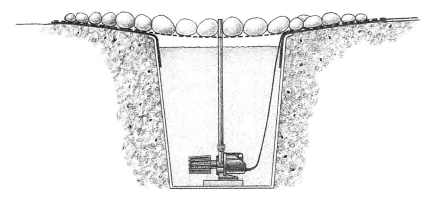

Permanent planting beds

Most of the planting in small to medium-sized pools is contained in wide-bottomed, open-meshed plastic planting crates of different sizes and shapes which sit either on the marginal shelves or on the pool bottom. They have the advantages of containing the very rapid growth of aquatics within manageable limits and allowing a planting scheme to be easily altered. Their disadvantages are that without feeding or division the plants can soon become stunted, and on windy sites the tall-leaved marginal aquatics are easily blown over. Nor are containers the most attractive method of displaying aquatic plants. In clear water they can be conspicuous, particularly when the polypropylene (plastic) or burlap lining has been insufficiently trimmed and folds of the material emerge at the corners of the container.

The alternative to containers, particularly for the medium to large pool, is to provide permanent planting beds on the marginal shelves and on the bottom during construction. These will encourage stronger and more sustained growth of aquatics and allow for larger plant groups. As any mixed planting will eventually become more intermingled in permanent marginal planting beds, the vigorous species must be carefully controlled to prevent them from suppressing the more dwarf forms.

The planting beds on the pool bottom will be used for the deeper-water aquatics such as water lilies and their size will depend on the overall depth and size of the pool. Vigorous water lilies in large pools, for instance, will need planting beds 2 ft. across and 15–18 in. deep. Medium-sized water lilies will need smaller planting beds, about 15–18 in. across and 15 in. deep.

A variety of materials can be used to create the side walls of the planting beds, such as bricks, concrete blocks or rocks. Water-resistant dark-colored bricks make excellent submerged walls, their dark bluish color merging well into the depths of the water. The same building materials are used to make the walls for the permanent planting beds along the marginal shelves.

Ready-made containers can, alternatively, be adapted to accommodate vigorous plants in large pools, such as plastic trash cans with their sides reduced in height, half plastic barrels and sections of large-diameter concrete pipes. Holes drilled in the sides of containers will increase gaseous exchange in the submerged soil. For smaller pools, large washing-up bowls can be used. For planting both permanent beds and plastic crates, see the next chapter, page 62.

Making permanent planting beds

To minimize any risk of damage to the main liner, the walls of the planting beds on the bottom of the pool are constructed on a mortar foundation on top of spare offcuts of liner fixed to the main liner with dabs of mortar. The walls for permanent planting beds along the marginal shelves should be made during the initial pool construction (see page 35). To allow for the extra width of the retaining wall, make a wider marginal shelf, to contain a minimum soil width of 9 in. between the retaining wall and the pool side.

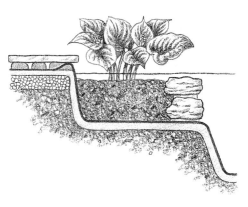

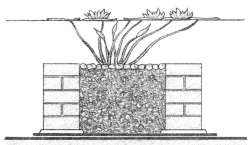

Build the retaining wall on the inside edge of the marginal shelf, finishing 3–4 in. below the water line.

Choosing and fitting a pump

Where you are installing any form of moving water, a pump will have to be fitted, and the most appropriate type and size requires careful consideration. There are two main types of electric pump available: surface-mounted pumps, which are needed for large waterfalls and fountains, and submersible pumps, which are adequate for smaller features.

Surface-mounted pumps

Surface-mounted pumps are most suitable for continuous running in larger water features, such as large fountains or extensive watercourses with high waterfalls, where greater water pressure is required. Surface-mounted electric pumps are all powered from the house and will need to be housed in a ventilated chamber, usually made of bricks or timber, which allows easy access for maintenance. All surface-mounted pumps have a specified maximum suction lift, and you should always take care to see that this maximum is not exceeded.

The pump should be placed close to the base pool so that the suction pipe to it is kept as short as possible. Flexible suction pipe must be of the reinforced type to prevent any buckling under the suction pressure. The delivery pipe should also be reinforced if it is buried in soil where a kink may occur through pressure from compaction of the soil.

If a surface-mounted pump is sited above the water level of the reservoir pool, a strainer and a one-way valve (which only allows the water to flow toward the pump and prevents the flow in the opposite direction) should be fitted to the end of the suction pipe, to eliminate the need for priming the pump after it has been turned off. If the pump is sited lower than the water level, this valve is not necessary, but a strainer should still be fitted.

Small submersible pumps can be used in a variety of innovative situations to create water movement. Here, a large glazed container has been adapted to make a raised pool; this is connected by a small pipe, through a watertight connection in the bottom, to a pump in the base pool. The recirculating water creates a small frothy spout and a rippling effect on the water surface. The healthy clump of arum lilies (Zantedeschia aethiopica) in the foreground is complemented by the contrasting foliage of the white dicentras and the blue-flowered bugle (Ajuga reptans).

Submersible pumps

Submersible pumps are much more convenient to install than surface-mounted pumps, requiring no special housing chamber or suction pipe. They can be obtained in 24-volt low voltage forms for small water features, although the majority of them are powered from the house (with a voltage of 115-volts). Submersible pumps have become increasingly reliable and efficient and for most domestic installations their convenience makes them more popular than surface-mounted pumps. They require little maintenance other than regular cleaning of the inlet filter, which may become choked up with debris or blanketweed. The installation of a submersible pump is illustrated on page 49.

Choosing the right size

Whatever type of pump you choose, its size, which is measured in an ouput of liters or gallons per hour, is determined by three main factors. First, you need to measure the height to which the water is to be lifted, referred to as the "head." In a fountain this would be the height beyond the jet or spout which the water is intended to reach; for a watercourse it would be the height at which the delivery pump discharges the water at the top of the watercourse. Second, you should measure the distance which the water will travel, a factor which is likely to be more relevant for a watercourse than a fountain. Third, you have to consider the diameter of the delivery pipe, which has a marked influence on the friction pressure exerted against the water. This is a major factor in the pump's output, which must be allowed for if the water is to be pumped long distances. A 2-in.-diameter pipe, for example, will have only a very small friction resistance compared to a domestic garden hose of approximately ½–¾ in. diameter.

Graphs and charts which take into account these factors are available at good suppliers to enable you to select the most suitable size of pump for the water feature you have in mind. Additionally, for waterfall installations, the width of the unbroken water curtain required to spill over the waterfall affects the size of pump, as do the number and types of jets fitted to any fountain.

Waterfalls

Pumps for waterfalls are required to deliver a large volume of water at low pressure, rather than a smaller volume of water at high pressure, as would be required for most types of fountain. They need to be quiet in running, particularly in small pools near a sitting area, so that the pleasure of the noise of moving water is not spoilt. For waterfalls which are to be kept running constantly, particularly those linked to a biological filter, ensure that the pump is suitable for continuous as against occasional use.

As a guide for waterfalls, a minimum of 1,135 liters (300 gallons) per hour is required to create an unbroken curtain of water 6 in. wide. In addition to this, the other factors mentioned above, such as height, distance and diameter of pipe, need to be taken into the calculation of the pump size.

The performance charts and output graphs supplied in certain mail order catalogs will help you make your choice, but it is generally a good idea to consult an expert for all but the simplest of waterfall features when buying the pump. It is usually better to choose on the side of over-capacity and to fit a gate valve to reduce the flow if it proves too powerful. Too much water changing quickly in the base pool is undesirable where there is a community of fish and plants, and the pump's hourly rate of change should not exceed the pool's total capacity. Once the various factors are known, the specialist supplier can recommend the minimum size of pump required for the system. A single pump can operate both a fountain and a waterfall by incorporating a T-junction into the delivery pipe. Gate valves are then fitted to each outlet beyond the junction to compensate for the different pressure required for each one.

The pump output port will give an indication of the diameter of flexible pipe which it is intended to fit without using a special adaptor. Where water is to be sent some distance, for instance, the friction loss in small-diameter pipes such as domestic hosepipes can be considerable and the pump's output is thereby reduced. Flexible pipes of 1¼–1½ in. diameter are recommended where the source of the waterfall is more than 17 ft. away from the base pool. Where possible, you should use reinforced pipework for these distances.

Fitting the pump

Waterproof connectors are available to connect the electricity from the pump to the house supply as the length of the cable supplied with a pump is unlikely to reach a suitable electric plug. These connectors are generally positioned under a rock or paving stone near the pool to enable the pump to be removed easily without disturbing a large length of cabling. The pump should always be raised off the bottom of the pool to prevent the pump intake from becoming clogged with organic matter.

Low-pressure submersible pumps for waterfalls are now sold in a wide variety of sizes. With only a relatively short drop down to the base pool, the unbroken curtain of water falling over this paving stone would require a minimum output of 2,500 liters per hour or 700 gallons. When choosing a pump, err on the side of over-capacity and fit a gate valve to reduce the flow if the fall of water is too turbulent.

Installing a submersible pump

Position the pump as close as possible to the bottom of a waterfall, where the water returns to the base pool. This reduces pipework to a minimum and prevents cross-currents and consequent temperature mixing in a small pool. Water lilies dislike any submerged currents or turbulence on the water surface, and it is better for fish and plants alike to have varying temperature layers in the different depths of water. Position the pump on a small ledge or on a raised base approximately 3–4 in. high.

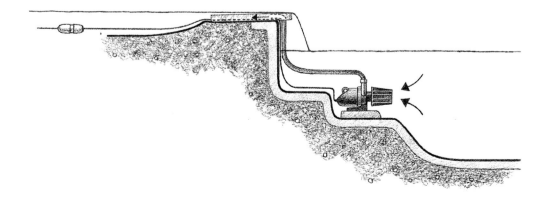

Introducing filtration

A combination of physical and biological filtration should be considered at the outset when designing a pool with fish. Rocks can be used to disguise the outlet of a filtration unit successfully.

Green water is the dread of many pool owners, and if it persists it can lead to frustration and a gradual loss of interest in the pool. Green water is likely to be experienced shortly after filling a new pool, particularly in mid-summer or following days of unbroken sunshine. After the crystal-clear condition as the pond is initially filled up, the water turns increasingly cloudy within two or three days. This is a perfectly natural process, caused by the explosion of myriad free-floating microscopic algae feeding on the rich supply of mineral salts in fresh tap water.

Starving out the food supply of the algae will remedy the condition in the long term, and this is achieved by introducing aquatic plants and letting them establish themselves. Competition for the food supply by submerged plants and shading out the light by surface-floating leaves will eventually show their joint effect, and the pool clarity will return

almost overnight as the plants become established.

Unfortunately there are occasions when the cloudy water persists, even where adequate planting has been undertaken. Some of the reasons for this persistence of cloudy water are explained in the chapter on pool problems, page 88, with suggestions for their control. But if the plant life within the pool is inadequate to perform a natural filtration process, or if the pool is to be used for high-stocking levels of ornamental fish, then it may prove necessary to introduce some form of filtration and this should, where possible, be considered at the time of construction.

Although there are recent developments in ultra-violet and ceramic filters, the more common forms of filter fall into two main categories, and both require a pump to circulate the water (see page 47). Physical or mechanical filters, which intercept particles of debris suspended in the water, are generally fitted to the intake of the pump and require frequent cleaning. The second type, biological filters, absorb the fish wastes that cause green water and harmful ammonia by encouraging the growth of beneficial bacteria inside the filter. In addition, associated microscopic organisms digest the algae. Once the harmful ammonia has been converted into non-toxic nitrates by the filter's bacteria, these are returned to the pool to be used by the plants.

Biological filters

It can take several weeks, sometimes months, for the bacteria in a biological filter to establish and get to work on the offending micro-organisms. Once running, these filters should not be turned off for significant periods or other harmful bacteria will develop, producing toxic hydrogen sulfide. They should even be kept running in all but the severest of winters. Before starting the filter up again after a long period of inactivity it will be essential to give it a thorough cleaning out.

Biological filters are bulky objects which are best built independently of the pool. As they need to be above the water level for the freshly filtered water to

return to the pool, some permanent disguise, by planting or positioning rocks will be necessary. As a guideline to the size required, a medium-sized pool well stocked with ornamental fish such as carp will need a prefabricated filter approximately the size of a domestic water tank.

Prefabricated filters have all the necessary fittings and valves for connecting pipework to make them easy to fit. They are, however, functional, unattractive intrusions on a water garden and a more acceptable alternative is to build a filter housing to fit the surroundings, using a liner and rock around the edges as if building a header pool for a stream or a raised pool. Instead of filling this raised pool with water, it is filled with a filter medium such as gravel. The freshly filtered water returns through submerged perforated pipes and is then piped or ducted up and over a waterfall just above the level of the filter medium. This ensures that the filter medium does not dry out if the pump is turned off, when the beneficial bacteria would be killed quickly. The surface of the filter pool could be disguised with rocks supported on a stout grid or mesh, for example made of timber and chicken wire, to blend it into the garden and make it less obtrusive.

An alternative method to a separate filter pool is to

build a submerged filtration system onto the bottom of the pool, as shown below. This system must be kept running continuously during the summer in order for the beneficial bacteria which grow on the gravel in the filter to thrive and be effective. If it is turned off for a day, the bacteria could die and would cause more harm than good.

Filtration is essential to maintain crystal-clear water in a pool stocked with ornamental large carp. Fully grown carp would disturb the roots of submerged aquatics.

Installing a submerged biological filter

A submerged filter combines the benefits of both mechanical and biological filters, and can be created during construction by building a container such as a large, submerged planting bed as described on page 46. The planting bed is filled with a porous medium, such as gravel, over a coil of perforated pipe connected to the intake of a submersible pump placed just outside the planting bed. The outlet of the pump discharges into the pond, waterfall or fountain, which then oxygenates the water.

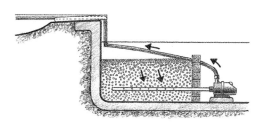

The water is drawn down into the coiled perforated pipe (shown in plan, right), then recirculated through the delivery pipe.

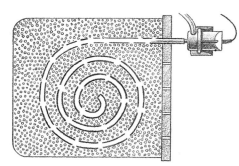

Streams and waterfalls

The installation of a circulating pump and the slightest change of level above the main pool creates the opportunity to include movement in the water garden. In a small garden, the simplest system requires no more than water pumped from the base pool to an adjacent pool at a slightly higher level; this water is then recirculated back to the base pool over a small waterfall. Streams and waterfalls can be created either by using preformed units or by means of a flexible liner.

Installing a preformed watercourse

One of the easiest ways of creating small sections of stream and a waterfall is to use prefabricated rigid or semi-rigid rock-pool and stream units. These are manufactured in fiberglass, plastic or PVC and are available from aquatic centers. Designed to carry water short distances over varying heights, each has a lip which overlaps the underlying unit. They are produced with a variety of simulated textures to their rocky edges to blend more naturally into the garden. But the edges look less artificial when disguised by rocks and softened with creeping plants.

RIGHT *Drumstick primulas* (Primula denticulata) *and marsh marigolds* (Caltha palustris) *grow in profusion along the sides of this rocky stream. The rocks along the edges, used to hide the liner and retain the soil, have quickly become covered in moss and seedling primulas have taken root, giving a more natural appearance.*

Choose a unit or mixture of units to suit the limitations of space and the availability of soil above the level of the main pool. Only the slightest of slopes is required for a watercourse and very few gardens are in fact dead-level. Once the units are on site, lay them on the surface in a variety of overlapping or interlocking positions until you are satisfied that you have achieved the most suitable layout.

The lip of a preformed stream or rock-pool unit should overlap the adjoining pool or the unit below it to provide an easy flow of water from level to level. The simplest arrangement would involve inserting a preformed pool at a higher level, creating a fall of water from it into the base pool at the lower level. Ensure that the unit in the excavated hole is dead level and that the lip overhangs the base pool.

More sophisticated designs incorporate long, narrow sections of shallow stream units installed as shown below on soft sand, their outlets overlapping rock pools at different levels, creating waterfalls. The stream units are prefabricated to ensure that, when installed level, some water is retained behind the stream outlets even when the pump is not running. They must be firmly backfilled along their sides.

At every change of level, ensure that there is adequate overlap from unit to unit to prevent any

Installing preformed units

With the units held temporarily in place on the site, mark out their outlines with bamboo canes or pegs. Put the units to one side and excavate the position of the lowest unit first. Make the excavation 2–3 in. deeper and wider than the size of the unit and line it with 2–3 in. of soft sand. Lay each unit on the base of soft sand, installing it by the same method as described for preformed pools on page 32. When installing the stream units, start from the edge of the bottom pool and work upward.

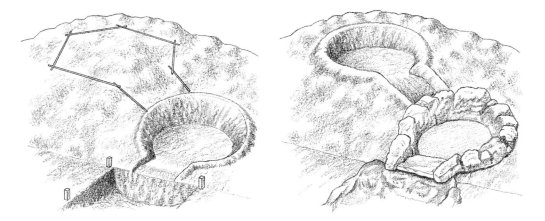

water being lost at the waterfalls. The vertical gap at the overlap of two units behind the waterfalls can be disguised with stone or rock. Test the flow of each section by using water from a garden hose before proceeding to the next level above. Where several stream units interconnect with rock pools, a more natural and interesting design is created when the streams vary in direction.

Once all the units are installed, a flexible pipe from the submersible pump in the bottom pool must be dug into a shallow trench running alongside the watercourse to emerge adjacent to, and spill into, the uppermost pool. It is better if the end of the outlet pipe is not submerged in the header pool, to prevent the pipe from acting as a siphon when the pump is turned off. But where it is difficult to disguise the outlet of the pipework from the pump into the header pool and it is therefore submerged, the pipe should be fitted with a one-way valve to prevent the water siphoning back down the pipe into the main pool when the pump is turned off.

To give greater rigidity to preformed waterfall units, particularly on made-up soil where future subsidence could affect the levels, heavy-duty inter-locking pools which bolt together are available with height-adjusting vertical plates between the pools.

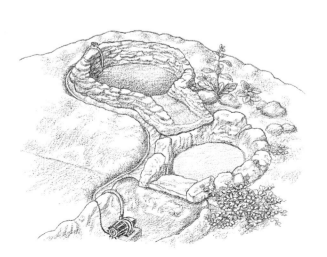

Installing a watercourse with a flexible liner

Flexible liners give greater freedom of design than preformed units and are much more easily disguised. Streams between waterfalls can be varied in length, width and direction, and by masking the edges with rocks, areas of wet soil can be created behind the rocks in order to grow marginal or moisture-loving plants. For extensive watercourses, where directional changes occur between the waterfalls, it is better to use several lengths of liner which overlap on the vertical falls than to make folds in one long piece of liner wherever the changes in direction occur.

The outline of the watercourse should first be marked out with bamboo canes, and pegs should be inserted where the waterfalls are proposed. Starting in the raised ground at the side of the base pool, dig out the course of the stream to the pegs, marking the base of the first waterfall, as shown below. Make a sill or ledge at the point where the water will return to the main pool to prevent the water from draining out of the stream when the pump is not operating. Spread a 1 in. layer of sand or place a layer of polyester matting or padding over the bottom of the trench before installing the liner.

If more than one length of liner is being used, drape the first length from below the water line in the base pool, along the length of the trench and over the vertical face of soil where the next waterfall will be made. Temporarily secure the liner in place before arranging the permanent edge of rocks which will form the stream sides. Lay these edging rocks onto a mortar base on top of the liner, leaving enough room on the outside of the rocks for soil to cover the liner between the rocks and the sides of the trench. This area, filled with permanently saturated soil, will form the planting area for the marginals.

Before building the waterfall, overlap the next piece of liner to be used for any higher stretches of stream over the liner already fitted, ensuring that the overlap occurs at the water level of the stream. If one long, continuous length of liner is used for the whole watercourse, the liner is draped loosely upstream until it can be installed permanently as work proceeds from the bottom.

Depending on the height of the waterfall, you may need to build rocks on top of each other to make a vertical face; build them on top of a base foundation of mortar and spare offcut of liner to protect the stream liner from damage. The backs of the rocks should be positioned so that they hide the vertical face of the overlapping liners.

At the height where the water will spill from the upper level, select a flattish rock, which will later channel the water, to sit between two larger flanking stones. This flattish rock should overlap the vertical

Large pieces of limestone have been used to great effect in the making of this watercourse, constructed in less than three weeks for a horticultural show. The placing of each stone is a work of art, not only on the base of the watercourse, but in the surrounding specimen rocks, positioned to disguise the flexible liner.

Excavating the stream

Make the excavation in the form of a flat-bottomed trench 4–6 in. deep at the end nearest the base pool and 12–15 in. at the furthest end. Take out the shallow trench 15–18 in. wider on each side than the proposed width of the stream, and with slightly angled sides. From the sill or ledge, dig out the bottom of the trench in a gradual slope away from the sill to deepen the depth of water held in the stream. Rake over the soil in the bottom of the trench, removing any sharp stones.

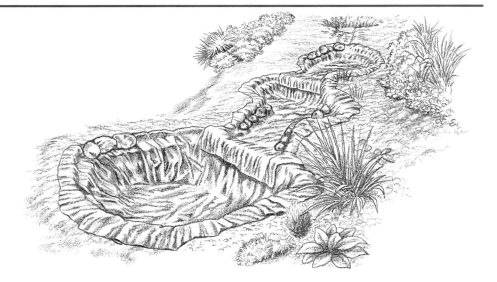

face of the rock wall by 2–3 in. in order for the water to fall clear of the rock face. Further rocks, which form the edge of the stream at the top of the waterfall, are mortared to the two flanking rocks at the top of the waterfall to create a watertight seal and channel the water over the fall. Use mortar to seal the joints between the liner and the rock at the top of the waterfall to prevent any inadvertent seepage of water behind the rock.

Repeat this process for as many stretches of stream or waterfall as required, varying the direction and width of the streams to add interest. Where the stream can be made wide enough for a rock to be placed in the center, the consequent funneling of water around the rock's side creates more rapid movement and greater interest.

At the highest point of the watercourse a small pool has to be formed, which is called the header pool. This collects the water from the outlet pipe of the circulating pump to form the water source for a system of streams and waterfalls, rather than a pipe simply emerging at the top of a stream. The outlet pipe from the circulating pump is fed out of the bottom pool and buried in a shallow trench alongside the watercourse until it emerges at the header pool. Where this pipe is fed over the sides of pools it is disguised by rock or stone.

Finally check the watercourse with the pump running for an hour or two, in case any water leaks over the sides of the liner, before finally covering the liner with soil along the sides of the stream above the water level. There is a danger that even a small amount of lime from the mortar between the rocks may affect the alkalinity of the watercourse and bottom pool. As a precaution against excess alkalinity, fill the system with a dilution of household vinegar at a ratio of 1:200. After leaving this dilution in the water for several days, rinse it out again and carefully paint over any large areas of exposed mortar with a brand-name sealant.

When the watercourse is brought into regular use, you should gradually increase the rate of flow to the desired level by adjusting a gate valve on the outlet pipe. This valve should be hidden under a rock near the header pool in a convenient place to enable adjustments to be made easily.

A watercourse set into a lawn

A lawn with only the slightest slope provides an opportunity to create a natural-looking stream with a rocky header pool. The header pool is approximately 3–5 ft. in diameter and the stream is 1–1½ ft. wide and approximately 23 ft. long. The informal pool at the lowest point is 6½–8 ft. in diameter, and is given emphasis by the bold leaves of *Gunnera manicata* planted in the moist soil near its edges. Rocks and creeping plants hide the circulating pipe from the submersible pump in the lower pool and cobble stones are grouped in the stream to create ripples on the moving water surface. Paving stones provide an informal path across the stream, with one wide stone secured by mortar onto the stream bottom. The stream affords scope to use specimen plants with large foliage such as the *Lysichiton camtschatcensis* with its bold, paddle-like leaves and the umbrella plant *(Darmera peltata)* with its attractive display of early-spring flowers and tall leaves. This water feature is shown as late spring advances into early summer.

1 *Ajuga reptans*: a carpeting, moisture-loving herbaceous perennial with blue flowers in spring and early summer; it is useful for scrambling over the edges of rocks and streams. It grows to only 6 in.

2 *Primula rosea*: a moisture-loving herbaceous perennial whose pink, polyanthus-like early spring flowers are carried on short stems above oval- to lance-shaped leaves, flushed bronze when young. It grows to 6 in.

3 *Caltha leptosepala*: a white-flowering species, similar to the common marsh marigold, this spring-flowering marginal grows in water 6 in. deep. It grows to 1 ft.

4 *Darmera peltata*: a striking, moisture-loving plant which is excellent for the sides of streams, where its surface rhizomes help to bind any loose earth. It has large, plate-like leaves held on tall stems and pinkish-white flowers,

appearing first, carried on long stems in early-spring. It grows to 3 ft.

5 *Eriophorum angustifolium*: a spreading marginal aquatic for shallow water or boggy soil with stiff, coarse, grassy foliage and tassels of white, cotton-wool-like flowers in mid- to late summer. It grows to 1 ft.

6 *Osmunda regalis*: a moisture-loving fern which looks good at the streamside throughout the seasons. In spring the furled fronds, like shepherds' crooks, are followed by bright green, pinnate fronds which turn rusty-red in the autumn. It grows to 6 ft.

7 *Primula florindae*: a vigorous primula for moist or wet soil which has several heads of large, sulfur-yellow, drooping, bell-like flowers dusted with farina. Its large, almost heart-shaped leaves can reach 8 in. long. It grows to 2½ ft.

8 *Iris laevigata*: an elegant marginal aquatic with sword-shaped, smooth leaves and blue flowers in mid-summer. It grows to 3 ft. Water depth: up to 4 in.

9 *Sagittaria sagittifolia*: a vigorous, spreading marginal aquatic with long, arrow-shaped, shiny leaves and tiers of white-petaled flowers with a purple blotch which appear in late summer. It grows to 1½ ft. Water depth: up to 9–12 in.

10 *Gunnera manicata*: a huge, moisture-loving, herbaceous perennial with distinctive, deeply lobed leaves, which can reach 5 ft. across, on thorny leaf stalks. Spikes of brown flowers produced in mid-summer are relatively inconspicuous between the massive leaves. It can grow to 6½ ft.

11 *Iris sibirica*: a moisture-loving iris with thin, grassy leaves and branched heads of blue-

or purple-veined flowers. It is a graceful plant, growing to a height of 4 ft.

12 *Veronica beccabunga*: a creeping marginal aquatic for shallow water, where its succulent stems scramble over the sides of a pool, producing blue flowers with white centers in spring and summer. It grows to 4 in.

13 *Lysichiton camtschatcensis*: a distinctive marginal aquatic for shallow water or deep boggy soil, where it produces bold, paddle-shaped leaves and impressive white, arum-like flowers in spring. It grows to 4 ft.

14 *Typha minima*: a charming small marginal aquatic for shallow water with needle-like leaves. The brown flower-heads are produced in late summer. It grows to 1½ ft.

15 *Primula bulleyana*: a candelabra-flowering primula for the moist margins of a stream or pool. It produces spikes of orange-yellow flowers in mid-summer carried in whorls on flower stems above thin, toothed oblong leaves. It grows to 3 ft.

16 *Iris pseudacorus* 'Variegata': a vigorous marginal aquatic producing yellow flowers in spring and early summer among distinctive, sword-shaped leaves, boldly striped in cream and green. The leaves, which grow to 3 ft., lose their variegation during summer.

17 *Primula pulverulenta*: an elegant, waterside, candelabra-type primula which produces bold tiers of rich crimson, purple-eyed flowers in late spring above lance-shaped, toothed leaves. It grows to 2 ft.

18 *Lysimachia nummularia*: a creeping moisture-lover which scrambles over stream or pool edges and produces small yellow, cup-shaped flowers in summer among the pairs of rounded leaves. It grows to 2 in.

19 *Leucojum aestivum*: a hardy bulb for moist soils which looks decorative by the waterside where the lush leaves produced in early-spring are followed by white, bell-shaped flowers tipped with green. It grows to 2 ft.

Bog gardens

Lythrum salicaria
Sometimes referred to as salicaria because of its slight resemblance to willow, the astringent qualities of purple loosestrife have long been recognized and used as an intestinal disinfectant. It is also a hair dye for blondness. Cross-pollination by bees and the consequent vigor of the species is ensured by the flower structure varying slightly from plant to plant in such a way that only pollen dust from neighboring plants reaches the stigmas. The species is such a prolific grower that planting it is banned in many states of North America.

Bog gardens are areas of saturated soil in which the plants known as marginal aquatics flourish. They are normally sited adjacent to an area of informal water but can be constructed at the same time as the pool or independently. Bog gardens are not suitable for the plants referred to as moisture-loving, which prefer permanently moist but drained soil.

Flexible liners allow bog gardens to be built alongside the pool by extending the liner and creating a barrier which lets water permeate the soil but at the same time prevents soil from falling into the pool. Bog gardens lose a large volume of water by evaporation from the soil surface and transpiration from the leaves. This inevitably causes a marked drop in the water level of any linked pool in dry, hot periods, which will necessitate frequent topping off. But regular top-offs with mains tap water containing a high mineral-salt level will alter the water chemistry dramatically if too much is added. So a large bog garden should not be linked to a small pool requiring constant replenishment of water.

A bog garden made with an independent liner allows greater flexibility in siting and shape. As the liner is completely covered with soil and not exposed to deterioration through ultraviolet light, cheaper materials like polyethylene can be used.

Creating an independent bog garden

Having defined the area for your bog garden, dig out the topsoil to a depth of 9 in. As the liner will be completely covered with soil, cheaper grades of membrane can be used, but since these cheap liners puncture easily, be sure that there are no sharp edges by raking over the area carefully. A small puncture is not a disaster in such a bed, however, as very slow seepage from the hole would hardly be noticed in boggy soils. Lay a protective mat of polyester padding over the bog area; then drape the main liner over it and temporarily anchor it at the sides by bricks or stones. If you are considering an automatic topping-off system (see below), install this before laying the padding and the liner.

As there is no water supply from an adjacent pool, the area will require frequent topping off manually by means of a hosepipe or a pipe buried into the bog area which has a hosepipe connector on the surface. Alternatively, a length of drip-irrigation hose could be laid on the surface and turned on in dry spells. Make this hose from a length of rigid alkathene or plastic pipe, stopped at one end and perforated with

Making a bog garden with an automatic topping-off system

Drape a liner into a hole 1½–2 ft. deep, which is connected by a rigid pipe through a watertight valve in the liner to an adjacent sunken water tank or cistern. The pipe inside the liner is perforated to allow water seepage and is surrounded by 2 in. of gravel to prevent soil from clogging the fine holes. The cistern is connected to the mains water supply, and the water maintained at a constant level, by a ballcock valve. Topsoil is returned to the bed once plumbing is done.

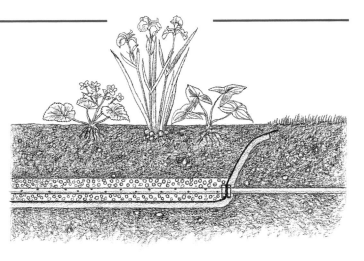

This small independent bog garden adjacent to a formal pool contains a comprehensive selection of moisture-loving plants, including astilbes, hostas and Ligularia dentata. The restriction of their roots in a relatively confined space will tend to suppress the vigorous growth of plants like Gunnera manicata, which would soon take over such a small area if given a free root run and ample moisture. To prevent its taking over, and shading out the hostas and other species, contain the Gunnera in a large pot. Blue and white cultivars of Iris sibirica are seen here flowering in early-summer.

⅛ in. diameter holes at 6 in. intervals along its length. Bury this in soil, having covered it with chippings to prevent the holes from being clogged up. A right-angle joint attaches another length of the same pipe to emerge above the soil surface with an adaptor to connect to a garden hose.

Completely automatic topping off could be provided through a small cistern for an area of soil independent of a pool that has to be kept permanently wet. The water supplied from the mains is maintained by a ballcock valve alongside the bed, with the float valve at the level of the water in the bog.

By puncturing the bog garden liner with a few small holes and covering the holes with chippings, you allow slow drainage, creating a bed for moisture-loving or marshland plants rather than for bog plants.

As the moisture level of a bog garden drops, water is automatically supplied to it from the sunken cistern (below).

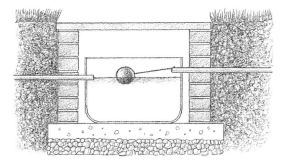

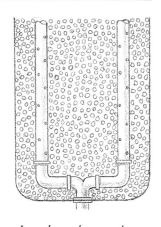

In a large bog garden, two lengths of pipe can be used.

59

Making a bog garden linked to a pool

In the initial design of the pool, an area beyond the proposed water's edge is marked out for the adjacent bog garden. As the liner is normally ordered in a rectangular shape, it will be necessary to make additions to the length or width of the liner (see page 30), or to both measurements if the bog garden surrounds two sides of the pool. When the excavation of the pool is started, the bog area can be created in one of two ways, as described below.

Forming a wall in the pool

Dig out the bog area to the same depth as the marginal shelf of the main pool, normally 9 in. Stack the topsoil nearby as you will need it to refill the bog area after installing the liner. Rake over the bog area and check for any sharp surfaces, in the same way as the main pool was prepared, then place a cushioning layer of polyester matting in the bottom. After installing the liner, making certain that the top edge is higher than the pool's water level, construct a dividing wall of bricks or walling stones along the line between pool and bog garden as shown on page 46. The base of the dividing wall should be mortared onto a spare offcut of liner to minimize any damage to the main liner. The top of this dividing wall

Creating a wall below the liner

Before installing the liner, take off 2–3 in. of soil from the top of the wall so that its finished height is below the proposed water line. Rake the base and walls of the bog area and remove any sharp materials prior to placing a cushioning laying of polyester matting over the whole surface, including the dividing earth ridge. Then install the liner, draping it over the ridge. Return the temporarily stored topsoil to the bog area, ensuring the liner's edge is above the water line before covering it completely with soil.

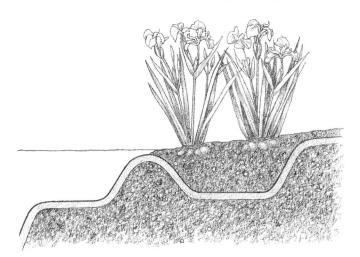

ABOVE LEFT *Dappled sunshine highlights the bold, broad leaves of the skunk cabbage* (Lysichiton americanus), *which make a striking contrast to the sword-like leaves of flag iris* (Iris pseudacorus).

RIGHT Iris sibirica *and* Primula pulverulenta *thrive in this bed of moisture-lovers, separated from the pool by a timber-topped retaining wall.*

should finish 2–3 in. below the proposed water level. The wall should be mortared between units to make it sufficiently rigid to resist the opposing pressures of water and wet soil.

Once the mortar has hardened, after a day or two, return the topsoil to the excavated area to a level just above the edge of the liner. Inverted rotting pieces of sod are good for disguisimg the top of the wall as they remain in place when the pool is filled.

Making the dividing wall below the liner

This method involves digging out the proposed bog area to a depth of 9 in. but leaving a ridge or wall of undisturbed soil about 1 ft. wide along the dividing line between the pool and bog area. The sides of this earth wall will be stronger if they are sloped to create a wider base. When calculating the liner size, allow for this extra ridge by adding twice its depth to the length or width of the liner. Prepare the bog area and install the liner as shown below. Then return the topsoil to the bog.

For both systems of construction, you can place extra soil around the outside edge of the liner gradually, to increase the soil level above the water line. When this soil level reaches 6–12 in. above the water line, moisture-loving plants can be planted into it, which will allow their roots to be in oxygenated soil but their root tips to reach the reservoir of saturated soil beneath.

When planting the bog area it will be necessary to work from boards once the water has permeated the soil. As the area becomes completely waterlogged, the level of the soil tends to sink a little; extra soil will be needed to restore the finished level, which should be 3–4 in. above the water line.

As bog plants can quickly spread in such conditions, you should consider preparing individual pockets to suit the different requirements of each plant species. This can be done beforehand for both systems of constructing a bog garden, either by building internal retaining walls on the liner or by creating ridges and pockets of various depths under the liner beforehand. If no physical barrier is provided to prevent the rapid intermingling of the roots, you will need to trim back the vigorous species regularly, in order to control the planting.

61

PLANTING AND STOCKING THE WATER GARDEN

Planting a water garden provides an unusual and interesting challenge since it involves mixing a widely diverse group of plants with differing cultivation requirements in a relatively small space. And, unlike other areas of ornamental planting, a water garden includes submerged plants whose contribution is functional rather than ornamental. But the plants form only one part of the fascinating submerged life of a pond. Even without the deliberate introduction of any fish, the pool will soon attract creatures of all sizes and shapes, most of them adding to the rich biological balance of a water garden.

A swamp cypress (Taxodium distichum) *forms the specimen tree above an excellent mixture of moisture-loving plants, dominated by shuttlecock ferns,* (Matteuccia struthiopteris). *The shade cast on this pool gives ideal conditions for duckweed* (Lemna), *a small floating aquatic which can totally cover a pool if left unchecked.*

Planting the water garden

There is a seemingly endless variety of plants whose potential is fully realized in the presence of water. The range of leaf sizes displayed in a water garden includes the smallest foliage in the plant kingdom, that of the duckweeds (*Lemna* species), and some of the largest leaves grown in temperate climates, those of the *Gunnera* species. The shape and texture of aquatic leaves also provide great variation and lively contrasts, from the robust, thrusting, sword-like leaves of the irises to the plate-like, shiny leaves of the water lilies (*Nymphaea* species and cultivars) and pond lilies (*Nuphar* species).

Aquatic flowers are no less diverse and interesting. Water lilies have been a source of artistic inspiration for centuries, emerging from their dark and muddy origins to provide exquisitely graceful flowers whose spectrum of subtle colorings changes constantly during their brief display, opening and closing with the appearance and disappearance of the sun. In the pool margins you will find a delicacy of flowers among the rank foliage, where the water reflects the fragile and exotic blooms of plants such as the Japanese iris (*Iris ensata*, syn. *I. kaempferi*), with their paper-thin flowers in delightful shades of blue, pink and mauve. And in the moist, rather than wet, soil of the pool's outer reaches, some of the most beautiful herbaceous plants can be grown.

If the water garden is large enough, the planting selection may include woody-stemmed shrubs and trees whose outline and color are a joy when reflected. Several woody plants enjoy the reserves of water at the poolside and their value is extended into winter with the many-colored stems of shrubby dogwoods (*Cornus* species) and the catkins of willows (*Salix* species). Other suitable trees include: weeping willow (*Salix babylonica*), swamp cypress (*Taxodium distichum*), dawn redwood (*Metasequoia glyptostroboides*), Italian alder (*Alnus cordata*), gray alder (*A. incana*), river birch (*Betula nigra*) and silver birch (*B. pendula*). All specimen plants providing reflection will need ample growing room, and their overall proportions must be considered carefully if they are to remain in scale with the area of water surface.

Aquatic plants

Aquatic plants are grouped for convenience into the zones of water in which they flourish, namely: submerged oxygenating plants; submerged deep-water plants, floating plants, marginal plants and moisture-loving plants. The techniques for planting them are given on pages 74–81.

Submerged oxygenating plants

Plants with their leaves below the water are vital to a healthy pool although most of the species used as oxygenators are native plants with limited ornamental value. They tend to grow with numerous branched stems carrying whorls of small leaves which sometimes reach the water surface. In daylight they supplement oxygen levels, which is extremely beneficial to fish. Their great value in an ornamental pond is to feed on any dissolved mineral salts in the water, denying the algae their food source and reducing the likelihood of green water. The most commonly used oxygenating plants are listed, left.

Submerged deep-water plants

Deep-water plants add variety of form and color to the water surface but have limited use as oxygenators as most of their leaves are above the surface of the water. Water lilies are the most obvious choice for deep water, both for their aesthetic value and for their effectiveness in reducing the development of submerged algae through the shade cast by their leaves. Even the smallest pool or tub garden can be planted with the charming and tiny white-flowered water lily *Nymphaea* 'Pygmaea Alba,' whereas larger lakes are the ideal home for the star-like reflections of white water lilies, particularly *N.* 'Gladstoniana.' The delicate but outstanding cultivar *N.* 'Ray Davies' is one of the most beautiful water lilies for a color scheme of pastel shades with its double, shell-pink flowers and shiny, almost purple foliage.

There are species and cultivars of hardy water lily in most colors except blue to suit the varying depths of water up to 3 ft. Water lilies should not be

RIGHT *The leaf variegation of* Hosta 'Frances Williams' *picks up the glaucous tones of the water lily foliage and the many yellow hues which surround this pool, particularly* Mimulus lutea *and the pale lemon* Alchemilla mollis. *The ability of hostas to thrive, like the conifer at their side, in dry soil at the water's edge makes them a good choice where the liner has not been extended.*

BELOW *Two moisture-loving plants provide drama with their foliage:* Gunnera manicata *in the background and* Rheum palmatum *var.* tanguticum.

confused with pond lilies (*Nuphar* species). Although superficially alike, pond lilies are vigorous plants which generally grow in deeper water than water lilies and have larger, coarser leaves. They are most easily distinguished when in bloom, carrying a smaller, yellow, globe-like flower borne on strong stems above the water surface.

The charm and beauty of a water lily can be spoilt by selecting too vigorous a species or cultivar or by planting too many for the size of pool. The surface of a well-planted pool should not be dominated but occasionally broken by water lily foliage; at least half of the water's surface should be left entirely clear. Overplanting is exacerbated when the plants are not regularly divided. Water lilies in need of division (see page 84) are easily identified by crowded leaves which are thrust vertically above the water instead of lying horizontally on the surface. Overgrown water lilies have fewer flowers, and the few that are produced are often hidden in the foliage.

Although the predominant plants growing in the deeper water of a pool are water lilies, there is a small group of other plants which thrives in the zone of water deeper than 6 in. Where the pool is large enough, excellent alternatives include the sweet-smelling white flowers of the water hawthorn (*Aponogeton distachyos*) or the curious flowers of the golden club (*Orontium aquaticum*), which are held among leaves with a silvery, almost metallic sheen. Other suggestions include water violet (*Hottonia palustris*), water fringe (*Nymphoides peltata*) and Japanese pond lily (*Nuphar japonica*). Some of these alternative species will grow in water that is too cold or shaded for the sun-loving water lilies.

Floating plants

Floating plants are able to colonize large expanses of still and slow-moving water and serve a useful purpose in the early establishment of a pool by shading out light and feeding on the mineral salts to reduce the green algae population. Once established, however, they can become a nuisance rather than an attraction. In small pools surplus plants can be

In this richly planted streamside, the distinctive dark leaves of Ligularia dentata *(top center) contrast with the feathery foliage and white flowers of astilbes and the variegated* Carex *below. In the foreground are the fluffy, creamy-white spikes of* Filipendula ulmaria.

netted off easily, but floating plants should be introduced with caution for large surfaces of water. In cold and temperate climates the most common member of this group of aquatics is duckweed *(Lemna)*, a tiny, twin-leaved plant which is small enough to be carried on the feathers or feet of birds and can be introduced to an ornamental pond quite accidentally. It is a common sight on the relatively motionless dikes of marshland, where it provides excellent food for wildfowl. In some cases it can completely cover the water surface, giving the appearance of a closely cut lawn and surprising many a boisterous dog on exercise! Other floating plants include fairy moss *(Azolla caroliniana)*, frogbit *(Hydrocharis morsus-ranae)* and water soldier *(Stratiotes aloides)* (see also Key Plants, page 112).

In tropical climates there are common species of floating plants, the water hyacinth *(Eichhornia crassipes)* and the water lettuce *(Pistia stratiotes)*, both of which are regarded as extremely troublesome weeds

which swamp rivers and inland waterways. They make a valuable contribution to the water garden in temperate climates, however, since they are kept in check, although they seldom achieve the same impressive size reached in tropical waters. Both plants have an attractive and intricate network of fine feeding roots which make a wonderful refuge for fish fry, provided they are protected from frost.

Marginal plants

Marginal plants thrive in waterlogged conditions, either in shallow water 3–6 in. deep or in saturated soil. In formal water, marginal plants like *Iris laevigata* provide a welcome and striking contrast around the pool sides. Other non-invasive marginals include pickerel weed *(Pontederia cordata)*, white arrow arum *(Peltandra alba)* and arum lily *(Zantedeschia aethiopica)*. For informal water gardens, marginal plants are invaluable and in some cases, particularly in wildlife pools, they completely dominate the water feature. Marginal plants can spread with alarming speed, and for this reason many water gardeners choose to plant them in submerged containers (see page 83). Certain species like *Typha latifolia* are too invasive for the small to medium-sized water garden and may damage a pool liner with their sharply pointed roots.

The majority of marginals form an attractive framework to a water garden, providing a colorful variety of robust foliage. An effective combination might consist of the tall, thin cylindrical stems of the variegated bulrush *(Schoenoplectus lacustris* 'Albescens') next to the plate-like leaves of the umbrella plant *(Darmera peltata)*, with their feet surrounded by the creeping, almost evergreen succulent stems of brooklime *(Veronica beccabunga)* with its charming pale blue, white-centered flowers.

Moisture-loving plants

These plants are sometimes erroneously referred to as bog plants, a term which is more appropriate to marginal plants. They differ from marginals in requiring a moist but well-drained soil and would not thrive if grown in waterlogged conditions. Moisture-lovers include a rich diversity of plants on the fringe of the water garden, from plants with

The glaucous blue foliage of Hosta sieboldiana *'Elegans' complements the deep purple tones of the flowers of the adjacent* Iris ensata. *The value of* Alchemilla mollis *flowers in providing a contrast to the shades of blue and violet is particularly well exploited in this poolside planting.*

dramatic leaves like giant rhubarb *(Rheum palmatum)* to the more compact members of the primrose family (Primulaceae), such as *Primula rosea* and *P. vialii*. In an ornamental garden an area of permanently moist soil is a resource to indulge and there are many species of dramatic and colorful herbaceous plants, such as hostas, day lilies *(Hemerocallis)*, lobelias and *Crocosmia*, which will amply reward the bonus of constant water supply with a prolific and attractive display of flower and foliage.

As the foliage of most water plants in temperate climates dies down in the winter, it is the moisture-loving woody shrubs and trees that give a framework to a planting scheme throughout the year. There is a surprisingly extensive selection of ornamental trees and shrubs which thrive in moist soil, including species of birch *(Betula)*, alder *(Alnus)*, blueberry *(Vaccinium)*, swamp cypress *(Taxodium)*, marsh rosemary *(Andromeda)*, poplar *(Populus)*, bamboo *(Arundinaria)* and sweet gale *(Myrica gale)*.

LEFT *A tapestry of form and color in a small space includes the large leaves of* Rheum palmatum *in the background, and the intense, almost purple leaf coloring of* Lobelia splendens *in the foreground.*

Planning the planting

With such an extensive range of plants at the water gardener's disposal, it is well worth preparing a planting scheme, especially as the rate of growth is so considerable, even in one year. Too many aspiring water gardeners are content to select at random from the stock displayed at an aquatic center. The size of available young plants may at first appear disappointingly small, but as the growth rate in and around water is so rapid, there is no point in seeking large specimens for instant effect. The main requirement is to create a good mix of foliage and not to overcrowd any areas of the pool with too many plants of the same growth habit.

Once you have drawn the outline of the pool (see page 70), you can draw up lists of appealing plants, using the information given in the chapter on Key Plants (see page 106), as well as suggestions found in aquatic catalogs. Even the most experienced designer will find such lists helpful as a memory aid when producing a planting plan. Where you are sufficiently knowledgeable about the plants' characteristics, a simple list of names is adequate, but where you are not familiar with the plants, you should supplement the list with notes on height, flower color, spread and leaf shape, to enable you to use each plant's full potential. Knowing the ultimate height of a plant is important, particularly when they are all of a similar size in small pots at planting time. It is easy to make the mistake of positioning plants where they will later block the view of the water's surface or choosing plants which will all too soon become out of proportion with the pool's surface area. For certain sites it will be useful to know whether the plants are shade- and wind-tolerant.

Visiting as many water gardens as possible, where the plants are labeled, is an invaluable way of supplementing the information given in the chapter on Key Plants. Make notes of your favorite species, with brief descriptions of the main characteristics, including the color and texture of the leaves. Time spent on observing individual plants and their neighbors will enable you to compile a personal plant catalog which will help enormously when selecting from the lists supplied in books or printed catalogs.

RIGHT *A profoundly pleasing combination of color shades is provided by this group of candelabra primulas which have produced several self-sown seedlings in the moist soil. The yellow flowers and bold, variegated sword-shaped leaves of* Iris pseudacorus *'Variegata' are seen to best effect when caught by the intense light of early-summer sunshine.*

ABOVE LEFT *The handsome, deeply cut leaves of giant rhubarb* (Rheum palmatum) *make it a striking waterside plant. It is underplanted here with the water forget-me-not* (Myosotis scorpioides), *with a variegated iris for contrast, seen in the background.*

BELOW LEFT *The pale violet flowers and variegated foliage make* Iris pallida *'Variegata' an excellent partner to* Primula pulverulenta *along the sides of this rocky stream.*

Take particular note of plant groupings and how successful they are; where a particular combination appeals to you, there is no reason why you should not simply copy it until you have built up more confidence and expertise. Choosing the right plant for a certain place is one of the pleasures of creative gardening. The fringes of a water garden provide a fertile platform to experiment with plant grouping, as successes and failures will become apparent very soon; they will not require several seasons to reach maturity.

There will be no need to mark on the plan the positions or names of the oxygenating plants as it is a simple matter of buying a mixture of the available species and spreading them evenly over the pool bottom. There are nine or ten commonly used oxygenators (see the list on page 64) and planting should contain at least one third of the available species, to ensure against certain types not thriving. Oxygenators are sold as unrooted bunches of stems and you need to allow one bunch for every sq. ft. of water surface.

Positioning the plants

As a general rule, work from the deep, central area of the pool outward, so the first group of plants to mark on the plan will be the deep-water aquatics, usually water lilies.

Deep-water aquatics There are water lilies suitable for every size of pond up to the larger lakes of 3 ft. depth. Make your choice to include a favorite color or selection of colors, and mark the outline of their eventual spread by drawing a circle to the corresponding scale. Resist the temptation to overplant, leaving at least half the water's surface free of foliage. Alternatives to water lilies are on page 111.

Marginal plants These shallow-water plants will be next for consideration. Single specimens of plants like marsh marigold *(Caltha palustris)*, water forget-me-not *(Myosotis palustris)* and water plantain *(Alisma plantago-aquatica)* may be appropriate for small pools, but for medium and large pools from 50 sq. ft. upward, planting in groups looks more effective. Taller specimens of marginal plant, such as bulrushes *(Schoenoplectus lacustris)*, flag iris *(Iris pseudacorus)* and sweet flag *(Acorus calamus)*, should be kept to the far side of the water, with only the occasional use of spiky, medium-sized leaves—of, for example, water plantain, arrow arum *(Peltandra sagittifolia)* and arrowhead *(Sagittaria sagittifolia)*—to break the foreground.

Variegated foliage is very effective when reflected and an occasional clump of creamy striped foliage like that of *Iris laevigata* 'Variegata,' *Glyceria maxima* var. *variegata* and *Acorus calamus* 'Variegatus' should be interspersed with the surrounding planting. Groups of the taller species should be kept separate by creating gaps between them in the planting, using carpeting or low-growing marginals such as brooklime *(Veronica beccabunga)* to grow in between.

From the descriptions of each plant's spread in the chapter on Key Plants, sketch in the outline of the marginals in pencil and to scale, on the plan. A picture will soon emerge of the pool and its surrounds which can be amended easily at this stage if it appears too overcrowded. Formal pools generally need less dense planting than informal pools. On the other hand, informal pools look better if you vary the allocation of space to each planting group, creating a more natural effect and the opportunity to mix a greater variety of species. In addition to creating as much interest as possible through a wide diversity in

foliage form, interest through flower color should be considered equally important. Many marginal plants flower quite early in the year, such as marsh marigolds, spearwort *(Ranunculus flammula)* and flag iris, and, like many other spring-flowering plants, they have mainly yellow blossoms. As there are several other aquatic plants, in a wider variety of colors, that flower later, the planting plan should aim to include species which maintain interest until late summer (see right).

Moisture-loving plants The moisture-lovers provide the final flourish to a water garden, challenging and extending the skill and art of the gardener. In these areas beyond the pool edge in informal gardens you should aim to achieve a harmonious mix of lush foliage and flower. The planting scheme will either relate to a particular viewpoint or be designed to be viewed from all sides. As more moisture-loving plants are added, the plan will become more interesting, as the link is formed between the water and the rest of the garden.

A reflective pool intended to be seen from a particular viewpoint enables an eye-catching specimen tree or shrub to be planted in a key position in the moisture-loving area (see the list of plants for reflection on page 14). The color or shape of this specimen may suggest good associate plants to surround and enhance it.

The intriguing bare flower stems of Darmera peltata *(formerly* Peltiphyllum peltatum) *emerge in early-spring from thick rhizomatous roots which stabilize the banks of streams and ponds. The young foliage is seen just emerging, to follow the flowers with its elegant umbrella-like leaves.*

LATE-FLOWERING AQUATICS AND MOISTURE-LOVERS
Alisma plantago-aquatica
  (water plantain)
Lobelia cardinalis
Lythrum salicaria
  (loosestrife)
Pontederia cordata
  (pickerel weed)
Sagittaria sagittifolia
  (arrowhead)
Typha minima

How to make a planting plan

First draw up a simple plan of the pool and surrounding area, using a scale of 1:20 for small ponds; larger schemes may need the scale reduced to 1:50 to get the whole area on the one plan. Plot on any relevant features, such as trees, or main viewpoints, like house windows or outdoor sitting areas to ensure that key reflective positions on the water surface are not obscured by other plants. Indicate the direction of the prevailing wind and factors which affect the degree of light and shade. Draw with a soft pencil.

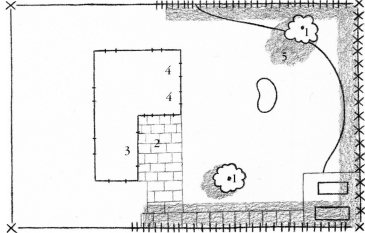

1 *Trees*
2 *Patio*
3 *Patio window*
4 *Living-room windows*
5 *Shade*

As there are, among moisture-loving plants, some with extremely large and striking leaves, these specimens must be given ample space to show off their beauty. Their immediate neighbors should therefore not be in competition but should be of a contrasting height and leaf form and preferably in flower at a different time. Like the marginal plants, most of the herbaceous moisture-lovers have limited winter interest, but this is more than compensated for by their lush growth and colorful displays in spring and summer. The interrelationship between the plants must take account of flower color in addition to height, leaf shape and texture. Achieving a successful combination of plants flowering at the same time is a skillful operation which justifies the time given to a planting plan. Fortunately, if any mistakes or color clashes occur, they are easily remedied by moving plants around during the following planting season.

Following the plan, the positions for plants beyond the pool edge can then be marked with bamboo canes or outlines of sand on the soil. As the water garden develops, its continual improvement will stimulate the gardener into learning about more plants and into visiting other gardens. As the need for increased planting space grows, it should be relatively easy to make more independent moisture-loving beds adjacent to the pool area without seriously affecting the main structure planting.

Positioning the plants on the plan

The deep-water aquatics are followed by the shallow-water marginals, and finally the moisture-lovers. As a general rule, plot the position of the largest specimens first. Use colored cardboard or tracing-paper discs cut to scale to represent each plant's spread. This makes it easy to shuffle plants around on the plan before finally penciling them in. If the colors of the discs represent those of the flowers, these will help in identifying good color combinations of plants flowering at the same time. Ink in the final planting plan.

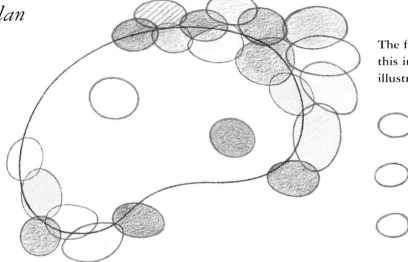

The final planting for this informal pool is illustrated on pages 72–3.

Deep-water aquatics

Shallow-water marginals

Moisture-lovers

An informal pool

This pool, which measures approximately 12 × 6 ft., is shown here in late summer, when many of the plants are at their best. The interest begins in the spring with marginals such as the giant marsh marigold *(Caltha palustris palustris,* syn. *C. polypetala)* with its large yellow flowers and the dramatic crimson flower spikes of the giant rhubarb *(Rheum palmatum* 'Atrosanguineum'*).* The plants also give a colorful autumn display of leaves and flowers, particularly the crimson-lipped flowers of *Lobelia* 'Queen Victoria,' and the creamy-white spikes of *Cimicifuga racemosa* 'Purpurea' held above the deeply divided purple leaves. The pool has a large enough water surface to reflect the nearby plants and contain the star-shaped blooms of the white water lily *(Nymphaea* 'Hermine'*)* and a profusion of the smaller, blood-red blooms of *Nymphaea* 'Froebelii.'

1 *Lobelia* 'Queen Victoria': a dramatic moisture-lover, with crimson-maroon foliage and velvety, scarlet flowers, which is slightly tender. It flowers in late summer in very shallow or moist conditions. It grows to 4ft.

2 *Scrophularia auriculata* 'Variegata': a moisture-loving perennial with striking, almost evergreen leaves with a broad band of cream. Inconspicuous purply maroon flowers appear in mid-summer. It grows to 3 ft.

3 *Pontederia cordata*: a shallow-water marginal aquatic with shiny, olive-green leaves standing erect on long stalks like spears. The soft blue flowers are held just above the leaves in late summer. It grows to 2 ft.

4 *Myosotis palustris*: a shallow-water marginal aquatic which scrambles over the pool edges and gives a prolific summer display of light blue flowers. It grows to 1 ft.

5 *Primula beesiana*: a moisture-loving herbaceous perennial with candelabra-type flower spikes in shades of pale mauve to deep carmine in spring to early summer. It grows to 2 ft.

6 *Polygonum bistorta*: a moisture-loving herbaceous perennial with soft pink poker-like flowers all summer above clumps of oblong leaves. It grows to 2½ ft.

7 *Butomus umbellatus*: a shallow-water marginal aquatic with thin, rush-like leaves and flowers in shell-pink umbels containing crimson stamens. It grows to 3 ft.

8 *Astilbe* 'Fanal': a moisture-lover with plumes of crimson flowers in summer above fern-like leaves. The old flowerheads persist into autumn. It grows to 2½ ft.

9 *Rheum palmatum* 'Atrosanguineum': this moisture-loving herbaceous perennial has impressive tall spikes of red flowers in spring carried above large, deeply cut leaves with red undersides. It grows to 6 ft.

10 *Veronica beccabunga*: this is a scrambling marginal aquatic which has succulent, almost evergreen stems and small blue flowers with white centers in spring and early summer. It grows 4 in. high.

11 *Cimicifuga racemosa* 'Purpurea': a moisture-lover with heavily scented, creamy-white

neat, round flowerheads of lilac to rich carmine-red which are held on stout stems above the lance-shaped leaves. It grows to 1 ft.

17 *Darmera peltata*: a distinctive moisture-lover which produces pink flowers on long stalks in early-spring before the umbrella-like leaves appear. The leaves turn to shades of russet and pink, deepening to burnt carmine, before the frosts. It grows to 3 ft.

18 *Menyanthes trifoliata*: a marginal aquatic with bean-like leaves that creep out over the water surface from the margins; they support fringed white flowers which can reach 9–16 in. above the water in early to mid-summer. The foliage is no higher than 8–10 in.

19 *Lysichiton americanus*: an architectural plant which is excellent for pool margins and streamsides, producing yellow arum-like flowers in early-spring and impressive paddle-like leaves. It grows to 3 ft.

20 *Peltandra sagittifolia*: a distinctive marginal with bright green, veined, arrow-shaped leaves and white, arum-like flowers in early summer, followed by clusters of red berries in autumn. It grows to 1½ ft.

21 *Nymphaea* 'Hermine': a profuse blooming white water lily with long-petaled, star-shaped flowers held just above the water. Water depth: 1–1½ ft.

22 *Nymphaea* 'Froebelii': a small-flowered water lily with tulip-shaped, blood-red flowers which are produced in profusion throughout the summer. Semi-erect leaves can grow 1 ft. above the water surface. It requires a water depth of 1–1½ ft.

23 *Orontium aquaticum*: a striking deep-water aquatic whose pencil-like, yellow-tipped white flowers look like small pokers; the bluish-green, lance-shaped leaves form a dense clump on the water surface. Semi-erect leaves can grow 1 ft. above the water surface. Water depth: 4–18 in.

bottle-brush flowers in autumn above deeply indented, almost crinkly purple leaves. It grows to 6 ft.

12 *Caltha palustris palustris*: this vigorous marginal aquatic has bright, shiny-yellow spring flowers held above a clump of rounded, dark green leaves. It grows to 2½ ft.

13 *Filipendula ulmaria* 'Aurea': a moisture-loving herbaceous perennial with creamy-white feathery flower spikes which are held above the deeply cut golden leaves in summer. It grows to 5 ft.

14 *Carex elata* 'Aurea': a shallow-water sedge grown for the impact of its long thin leaves, like dense tufts of yellow grass. The spring flowers are inconspicuous but the leaves last into autumn. It grows to 2 ft.

15 *Iris sibirica*: a graceful moisture-loving herbaceous iris with grass-like leaves. The branching heads of blue or purple early-summer flowers have yellow or white veining on the fall petals. It grows to 4 ft.

16 *Primula denticulata*: this moisture-loving perennial is a harbinger of spring, with its

Planting techniques

Nuphar lutea
The pond lily is a vigorous aquatic with the largest leaf of any British aquatic plant. Its other common name, brandy bottle, is derived from the resemblance of the seed capsule to a miniature whiskey bottle. Its reputation in classical medicine, that it removes the sexual drive, may have been the motive for carving its outline on the roof bosses of Westminster Abbey and Bristol Cathedral, to encourage clergy to celibacy.

Aquatic plants are normally planted between late spring and late summer, the earlier in the season the better. Unlike their terrestrial counterparts, they are unlikely to experience water stress after planting and during their establishment. Winter planting is not recommended as it could lead to rotting of any damaged tissue in submerged conditions.

There are two basic methods of planting aquatics: putting them into planting crates which are submerged after being planted, and planting them directly into submerged beds or into a layer of soil which covers the pond bottom.

Aquatic containers which are to be submerged are made of black rigid polyethylene or plastic; they have permeable latticework or louver-like sides which enable the movement of water and gases between the compost inside the container and the surrounding water. The containers come in square, rounded or curving shapes, ranging from 5–12 in. square and 4–8 in. deep. Larger tub-like containers are available for vigorous water lilies. They all have a wide, flat base to give stability and the square ones have sloping sides to fit snugly against the pool walls. Containers with latticework sides, having larger holes in the plastic, need to be lined with squares of permeable material like burlap or polypro-

pylene to help prevent compost and roots escaping from the sides. The herringbone-design and louvered containers have such fine holes that there is no need to line the sides first.

Making use of aquatic containers gives greater control over the planting and allows for easier removal of plants. Vigorous species can soon become stunted in containers and, where this occurs, the plants should be regularly divided and fed with special aquatic fertilizer tablets as described in the next chapter (see page 84).

For larger pools or those constructed as wildlife pools, plant directly into specially constructed beds, as described on page 44, or into a layer of soil covering the pool liner. As this free root-run encourages rapid intermixing of adjoining species, care must be taken in the arrangement of the planting and encroaching species should be cut back.

The planting medium

If the existing garden soil is not sand and has a pH value of between 6.5 and 7.0, it will probably be adequate as a planting medium for aquatics. Sandy soil is unsuitable since it contains insufficient nutrients for sustained aquatic growth. A soil containing a large proportion of organic matter is likely to give

---

Planting oxygenators in containers

Fill the container almost level with soil or compost and insert the bunches into holes made in the compost with a dibble. Ensure that the lead wire or weight is properly buried in the compost. Once the bunches are inserted, firm the compost thoroughly and lay a covering of small chippings or washed pea gravel on top to prevent loose particles of compost from floating away when the container is submerged. Water thoroughly to dispel any air before placing the container on the bottom of the pond.

Trim the bunches level and clasp them together with a piece of lead.

Make holes with a round stick slightly thicker than a pencil.

Cover the compost with a layer of washed pea gravel or chippings.

off methane gas as the organic matter decomposes, and a proportion of the methane gas is later absorbed by the water—which is toxic to fish. A rough idea of the soil's consistency can be obtained by shaking up a sample of soil in a glass jar half full of water and leaving it for a few days. The heavier sand particles will settle out below the finer clay layer. In a soil that is too sandy, these larger sand particles, which are the first to settle out, will make up more than one third of the total soil sample. The finer clay particles settle out later, above the sand layer, and these should dominate a garden soil suitable for aquatics.

Before using garden soil in a pool, ensure that it has not been recently enriched with fertilizer and bulky organic manures, or treated with insecticide or herbicide. Well-fertilized soils will leach out nutrients into the pond water, resulting in the increased growth of algae. Sieve out any stones or the roots of perennial weeds from the soil before using it.

Aquatic compost can be bought at most aquatic centers in sealed bags. It is extremely variable in quality and should only be bought from a reputable source. Examine the consistency of the compost before purchasing it, by asking for a bag to be opened so that you can ensure that it is loam-based and that there is no apparent sign of peat or evidence of larger sand particles.

Planting oxygenators

Oxygenators are the first group to be planted into a new pool. It is best to mix at least three or four species of oxygenator in case the water chemistry does not suit one particular species. Bunches can be mixed in the same planting crate or planted separately, with one species to each container, if the pool size requires several containers. Ensure that the plants are clean and not full of duckweed.

Oxygenating plants are sold as bunches of unrooted cuttings 6–9 in. long and clasped together near the base with a small piece of lead to prevent them floating, if dislodged from the planting medium. In most small ponds they are planted in small to medium-sized aquatic containers. A medium-sized crate, approximately 4 in. square, will hold five bunches, one bunch planted in each corner and one in the center. Should it prove difficult to reach the bottom of the pool, you will need to enlist somebody's help to hold the ends of two strings which are threaded through the mesh sides or handles of the container. The container, supported by holding both ends of the strings, can then be gently lowered into the water. After releasing the strings at one end, they can easily be pulled back through the sides and out of the water.

Alternatively, if the planting can coincide with filling the pool, you can place the containers on the bottom before the pool is deeper than the tops of calf- or knee-height rubber boots.

The pastel shades of the moisture-loving candelabra primulas are reflected by the fringe of young water lily leaves in the pool itself in early summer. As the flowers fade on the candelabras, the citrus-yellow spikes of the Himalayan cowslip (Primula florindae) follow at the very edge of the water. The brown fronds of the regal fern emerge among its pinnate foliage above the rock.

Planting water lilies

Most aquatic nurseries supply water lilies bare-rooted with the option of a few species and cultivars planted in containers. As there are basically two main types of hardy water lily root, you should examine the roots carefully before planting to see if they belong to the *Nymphaea odorata* type, which has horizontally growing, rhizomatous roots. Other cultivars have the more common vertically growing, log-like roots which have a ruff of finer roots emerging near the top, where the leaves appear.

In addition to the two main types of rootstock, there is considerable variation in the vigor of different water lilies, and the size of the container will need to be chosen with the potential growth in mind. At the two extremes of water lily vigor, the pygmy water lilies will need no more than a medium-sized planting crate which is 8 in. square, and the large, vigorous varieties will need small tubs with a minimum diameter of 14–16 in. But the majority of water lilies will be perfectly happy in large plastic planting crates approximately 1 ft. square, provided they are divided every three to four years (see page 84).

As water lilies are likely to remain in the planting crate for a minimum of three years, it is important to provide a firm compost in which they can root (see

below). Considerable shrinkage of the compost occurs when the container is immersed and the air is expelled, and it is not uncommon to see water lily roots struggling in containers barely half full after only a short time underwater.

The newly potted plant must not be kept out of the water longer than is absolutely necessary and should be planted in the pool without delay. If for

The floating stems of the bog bean (Menyanthes trifoliata) advance across the surface to greet the water lilies in late summer. The pink flower spikes are those of loosestrife (Lythrum salicaria).

Planting bare-rooted water lilies

Before planting the rootstock, thoroughly consolidate the compost in the container. Lay the horizontally growing rootstocks onto the firmed compost and cover them with 1 in. of soil, leaving the growing point exposed just above the surface. The more common log-like, upright rootstocks are planted vertically with the crown just exposed above the compost. The compost is covered with a layer of washed grit or pea gravel and gently watered. The planting crate is then immersed in the pool.

Trim off the old fibrous roots from the rootstock and most of any leaves which are present.

Plant the upright rootstock in the compost with the crown just exposed.

After planting, cover the compost with gravel and water the container before submerging it.

any reason planting in its permanent quarters is delayed, the freshly potted plant should be submerged into a bucket or container of water so that the roots are covered until it can be planted in the pool. The planting crate can be lowered into position by two people, one at each side of the pool, holding strong strings threaded through the water lily baskets and pulled out, once submerged in position, as shown for oxygenating plants (see page 74).

Containerized plants If water lilies have been purchased as containerized plants, it is unlikely that the container in which they are sold will be large enough for two to three years' subsequent growth. If the soil adheres well to the root when removing the container, the whole block of soil and roots should be replanted into a larger one, ensuring that the growing point is not buried. If the soil falls away from the root as the container is removed, planting procedure is the same as for bare-rooted plants.

Immersing

When positioning the freshly planted crate in the pool, it should be temporarily submerged to a shallow depth in order for the young leaves to reach the surface quickly and produce the vital food for the developing rootstock. Submerging the crate too deeply at planting time is the most common cause of failure in establishing new water lilies. This initial

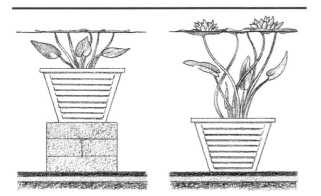

Young water lilies should be supported on temporary blocks until they are stronger.

The increased production of the surface leaves indicates that the blocks can be removed.

shallow planting is achieved by placing several bricks or walling blocks underneath the container so that the growing point is only 6–10 in. below the water surface. As more leaves develop and the plant grows stronger, the bricks are removed one by one until the plant is at its permanent depth.

An alternative method, which is also appropriate for any water lilies planted into submerged planting beds, is to keep the level of the pond to 6 in. above the newly positioned plants and gradually increase the depth of the pool to the final level as the plant strengthens. This system would also be more viable where it is difficult to remove bricks from the temporarily submerged supports as the plant grows, because the final water level of the pool is too deep for easy access.

In certain situations, particularly for large wildlife pools or deep lakes, water lilies may have to be dropped into the water to take root in the natural pool bottom. This involves planting water lily roots in burlap squares which have their corners tied loosely around the neck of the water lily. Sandbags which have one side slit to plant the water lily into compost inside the bag will also make a good container for dropping gently over the side of a boat.

The large round leaves and exquisite deep pink flowers of Nymphaea tuberosa *are shown off to full advantage against dark water. The generous spacing between the leaves, which seem to hug the water surface, greatly increases the attraction of this plant.*

A formal pool designed for reflections

This pool, featured in high summer, contains three beautiful water lily cultivars, which dominate the water surface and provide lovely reflections. Prominence is given to *Nymphaea* 'Escarboucle,' one of the most outstanding red water lilies with vermilion-red petals. This is flanked by two pink cultivars: *N.* 'Amabilis,' whose flowers, with their pointed petals and orange stamens, close quite late in the day and *N.* 'Firecrest,' a most reliable and prolific flowerer. The strap-like leaves and curious white flowers of the water hawthorn *(Aponogeton distachyos)* add further interest to the water surface. Symmetry is achieved through corner plantings, each of which has a centerpiece of strong vertical leaves, such as the *Iris* and the variegated bulrush *(Schoenoplectus lacustris* 'Albescens'). The pool measures approximately 16 × 10 ft. but the planting style could easily be adapted to a smaller pool by reducing the number of water lilies planted near the sides and leaving out the water hawthorn.

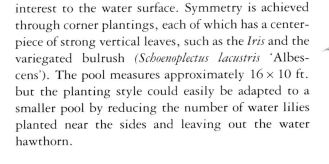

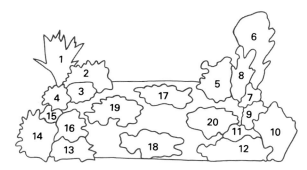

1 *Iris pseudacorus* 'Variegata': a vigorous marginal aquatic with strong, sword-shaped leaves and yellow flowers in spring. It grows to 3 ft.

2 *Peltandra sagittifolia*: a marginal aquatic with distinctive, bright green arrow-shaped leaves and white arum-like flowers. These are produced in spring and are followed by red berries. It grows to 1½ ft.

3 *Caltha palustris* 'Flore Pleno': a marginal aquatic producing masses of rounded, yellow flowers in spring which almost completely cover the foliage. It grows to 1 ft.

4 *Cotula coronopifolia*: a marginal aquatic with a bright display of rounded yellow flowers in mid-summer over tight mounds of succulent, scented foliage. It grows to 1 ft.

5 *Zantedeschia aethiopica*: a marginal which thrives in shallow, submerged conditions at the poolside, where it produces white trumpet flowers in high summer. These are held above deep green, shiny, arrow-shaped leaves. It grows to 2–3 ft.

6 *Schoenoplectus lacustris* 'Albescens': a distinctive marginal aquatic with erect, narrow cylindrical stems with variegated, creamy stripes and insignificant flowers. It grows to 3 ft.

7 *Veronica beccabunga*: a shallow-water, scrambling, marginal aquatic whose spreading, succulent, almost evergreen stems soften pool edges. The small blue flowers with white centers are produced in spring and early summer. It grows to 4 in.

8 *Iris laevigata*: an attractive shallow-water marginal with smooth green, sword-shaped leaves and exquisite blue flowers in summer. The many excellent cultivars provide a wide range of colors. It grows to 3 ft.

9 *Sagittaria sagittifolia* 'Flore Pleno': a marginal aquatic with slender, arrow-shaped upright leaves and specks of double white flowers in mid- to late summer. It grows to 3 ft.

10 *Iris laevigata* 'Variegata': one of the most attractive marginal plants, producing beautiful pale blue flowers above sword-shaped leaves which have a creamy, vertical banding. It grows to 3 ft.

11 *Myosotis palustris*: a shallow-water marginal aquatic whose semi-prostrate stems support a prolific display of light blue flowers with yellow centers in early summer. It grows to 1 ft.

12 *Mentha aquatica*: a spreading marginal aquatic producing whorls of axillary, lilac-colored flowers from the familiar mint stems and leaves. It grows to 3 ft.

13 *Houttuynia cordata* 'Flore Pleno': a spreading marginal aquatic with heart-shaped, bluish-green leaves and white feathers in mid- to late summer. It grows to 20 in.

14 *Pontederia cordata*: a shallow-water marginal aquatic with erect, long-stalked, shiny olive-green leaf blades and soft blue flowers in late summer. It grows to 2 ft.

15 *Myriophyllum aquaticum*: a submerged creeping aquatic whose soft stems emerge from shallow water and gently cover the edges of pools or tubs. The whorls of fine, light green foliage are at their most attractive in late summer.

16 *Saururus cernuus*: a marginal aquatic with bright green, heart-shaped leaves and nodding, creamy-white, scented flower spikes. It grows to 2 ft.

17 *Nymphaea* 'Amabilis': a pink water lily whose flat, star-like flowers have pointed petals and orange stamens. The young leaves change from dark red to olive-green. Water depth: 1–1½ ft.

18 *Nymphaea* 'Firecrest': a pink water lily whose dish-like flowers have bright orange stamens inside pale pink petals. Water depth: 1–1½ ft.

19 *Nymphaea* 'Escarboucle': a vigorous water lily whose large red fragrant flowers have vermilion-crimson petals and reddish stamens with yellow tips. The young leaves are a coppery shade, turning to mid-green. Water depth: 16–36 in.

20 *Aponogeton distachyos*: a submerged aquatic perennial which has a flush of fragrant white flowers with black anthers above the water in spring and autumn. The strap-like floating leaves contrast well with the rounder leaves of the water lilies. It requires a water depth of 9–30 in.

Planting marginals

Unlike water lilies, marginal aquatics are nearly always sold as containerized plants, unless they are supplied by mail order, which necessitates dispatching bare-rooted plants. As marginals can make considerable stem and leaf growth during the summer, they are best planted as early as possible in the aquatic planting season. If planted later in the summer, aerial growth should be cut back at planting time to help prevent windrock while the young roots of the marginals are trying to establish themselves in the soft, submerged compost.

Planting in containers Marginal aquatics are normally planted into medium-sized planting crates which have a diameter of 10 in. and depth of 5½ in. Very vigorous species will need the larger containers of 1 ft. diameter, provided the marginal shelf is sufficiently deep for their height, which is 8 in. The tops of containers should never be seen above the water surface. For speedier establishment, the large crates can be planted with two or three different plant species together in the same container.

If the marginal plants are planted into saturated soil outside the pool edge rather than underwater, the technique involves scooping out a planting hole large enough to contain the roots when they are removed from the old container, then inserting the plants and replacing soil around and over their roots, with a covering of no more than 1 in. On large beds it is better to work from wooden boards rather than trample on the waterlogged soil.

Planting into submerged beds Even if the pool is full of water it is relatively easy to reach the marginal planting beds at the sides in order to plant. Remove the plant from its pot and dig a hole the size of the pot in the submerged compost with a trowel. Insert the rootball in the hole and cover it with no more than 1 in. of soil, making sure that it is firmed in well to prevent it from becoming dislodged and floating away. Cover the area around the top of the plant's root system with washed pea gravel or with chippings.

Bare-rooted plants can be planted into either containers or planting beds, taking care not to bury them too deeply into the compost when planting. Freshly planted roots should always be covered with pea gravel or chippings, to prevent inquisitive fish from dislodging them before the roots have had time to anchor the plant firmly in the compost.

Planting floating plants

Floating plants need no more than to be placed on the water surface, either individually for large species like water hyacinth and water lettuce or by emptying out of a bag for the smaller species like duckweed or

Streams afford an excellent opportunity to plant a wide variety of marginal and moisture-loving plants in the varying levels of moisture along its length. The foliage of Caltha *and* Lysichiton *make a good partnership with the bright green ferns and the pinks and reds of the candelabra primulas nearby.*

Planting marginals in containers

Line a latticework crate with burlap or polypropylene-weave liners. Fill it with enough compacted aquatic compost or good garden soil so that when the pot containing the new plant is stood on the compost, its top is level with the top of the planting crate. Remove the plant from its pot and place it on the compacted compost. Add more compost, firming it around the sides and on top of the roots, to cover with no more than 1 in. of fresh compost. Cover with pea gravel and water thoroughly before submerging.

fairy moss. Wind tends to blow floating plants around the pool so the larger species should be placed in a sheltered position until they develop their new root systems. Water hyacinths may lie on their side for a while if they have been out of water for some time, but they will soon become upright again as the new roots of the plants start to grow.

Planting moisture-lovers

As these plants are planted into soil that is not saturated, they are treated in the same way as ordinary herbaceous plants. Most species are sold as containerized plants, which require making holes in the bed that are the same size and slightly deeper than the container. The young plant is then gently inserted into the hole after removing the pot. The soil is replaced and the surrounding soil should be firmed well afterward, taking care not to bury the growing point of the plant.

Planting wildlife pools

As stocking these "natural" pools requires planting into a layer of soil over the entire pool bottom (see page 36), it is better to do this as the pool is gradually filled, inserting the plants just before raising the water level to cover them. The new pool may well resemble a mud bath immediately after planting but the cloudiness caused by suspended soil particles will settle out in a few days. Bottom-dwelling fish which disturb the soil should not be introduced until the submerged oxygenating plants have formed a foothold and consolidated the soil.

A striking combination of texture, shape and color is seen in this plant association at the margins of the pool. The sword-like foliage of variegated flag iris (Iris pseudacorus 'Variegata') contrasts with that of the Indian club (Orontium aquaticum), with its curious pencil-like flower spikes. Both aquatics grow in water up to 15 in. deep.

A split-level formal pool with a waterfall

A raised pool offers many advantages on a patio. This pool, shown in early summer and measuring 8 × 8 ft., requires only limited excavation to the lower level to achieve the necessary depth for the water plants to survive the winter. The surrounding edge of the upper pool is high and wide enough to be used as a casual seat. The planting is restricted to the dramatic foliage of iris and bulrush, which complements the strong emphasis of the pool's outline. A pink water lily is planted at the lower level, where there is less risk of turbulence to the water surface from a fountain or water currents. The gentle water obstruction, created by a wide paving stone and used as the waterfall, provides a restful sound while hardly disturbing the water surface. A fountain can be turned on as required in the upper pool to give sound and extra movement on a hot, still day. A single pump operates the fountain and circulates the water flow over the water obstruction.

Clockwise from bottom-left corner of top pool:

1 *Azolla caroliniana*: a floating aquatic which will congregate in the corners of pools when there is any disturbance of the surface by a fountain or wind. It makes a nice break to the water surface with its dainty, fern-like leaves which turn red in the autumn.

2 *Iris pseudacorus* 'Variegata': a vigorous marginal aquatic with sword-shaped, boldly striped leaves and yellow flowers in spring and early summer. It grows to 3 ft.

3 *Schoenoplectus lacustris tabernaemontani* 'Zebrinus': a marginal aquatic with dramatic, rush-like leaves which have bold horizontal stripes; its compact shape makes the plant a useful architectural feature from early summer to autumn. It grows to 3 ft.

4 *Nymphaea* 'Pink Sensation': an outstanding pink water lily with long, oval-shaped petals which have a slightly deeper pink center and a silvery-pink sheen. Its fragrant flowers stay open well into the afternoon. It is a medium to strong grower. It requires a water depth of 1–1½ ft.

5 *Eichhornia crassipes*: a tender floating aquatic whose balloon-like petioles and shiny, kidney-shaped leaves are an intriguing sight on the water surface in summer. In very hot summers, it will produce spikes of pale blue to lilac flowers with yellow eyes. The long roots provide a refuge for fish fry and make a valuable oxygenator. It should be removed to a frost-free, moist soil or shallow water surface for the winter in temperate climates. Each clump grows to 9 in. and spreads 1 ft. across the water.

A water garden contained in a tub

Even a balcony or the smallest of terraces can be enlivened by the lushness of foliage in a water tub. This wooden half-barrel, 3 ft. in diameter, shown in late summer, is deep enough, at 1½ ft. high, to enable the miniature water lily to survive most temperate winters. It has enough submerged vegetation to provide oxygen for a pair of goldfish which will appreciate the shade given by the water lily leaves and a handful of fairy moss *(Azolla caroliniana)* in summer. The sides and edges of the tub are enhanced by one of the most delightful of creeping aquatics, parrot's feather *(Myriophyllum aquaticum)*, whose lovely soft stems gently curl and spill over the edges. Two intriguing plants, which bring the appeal of the larger poolside to this miniaturized landscape, are the contorted stemmed rush *(Juncus effusus* 'Spiralis') and the sleek miniature reedmace *(Typha minima)* with its tiny cylindrical leaves and its dark brown, soft baubles of flowers.

Clockwise from bottom left:

1 *Myriophyllum aquaticum*: a slightly tender marginal plant for shallow water which is excellent for enhancing the edges of tubs or small pools. Its fresh green, filigree foliage, borne on whorls of soft, curling stems, is at its best in mid- to late summer. Its spread across the water surface varies from 1 to 3 ft., depending on the regional climate in which it is grown.

2 *Typha minima*: a shallow-water marginal which has needle-like leaves and spherical, brown flowerheads. These are about the size of marbles and appear in late summer. It grows to 1½ ft.

3 *Juncus effusus* 'Spiralis': a shallow-water marginal with dark green, corkscrew-like, cylindrical leaves grown for its foliage effect from mid-summer onward. It grows to 1½ ft.

4 *Iris laevigata*: a shallow-water marginal aquatic with blue flowers in summer and sword-shaped, smooth leaves. It grows to 3 ft.

5 *Azolla caroliniana*: a floating aquatic whose dainty, fern-like leaves bring added mystery to the underwater world of a tub or small pool. It dies down in winter after turning pinkish-red and the over-wintering buds sink to the bottom; they float to the surface in spring, when the weather warms up.

6 *Nymphaea × helvola*: a miniature water lily whose soft-primrose, star-shaped flowers, only 2 in. in diameter, have orange stamens and are surrounded by dainty, attractively mottled, olive-green leaves. It spreads to no more than 1½ ft. Water depth: 6–9 in.

Propagating aquatics

Most aquatics can be propagated by division, seed or cuttings. The best method for individual plants is given in the chapter on Key Plants, page 106.

Division

In all but a few cases, marginals are most successfully propagated by division in spring or early summer. The main exceptions are *Alisma plantago-aquatica*, *Lysichiton americanus* and *L. camtschatcensis*. Separating pieces of the root system enables the outer or younger portions of the root to be replanted in fresh compost, after discarding the rest. Young plants with fibrous roots are divided by gently pulling them apart by hand, but as plants mature, a knife or spade may be necessary to cut or chop the root system into smaller pieces. In plants with thick rhizomes, such as iris, each cut section must contain at least one bud, and preferably some young fibrous roots.

Cut back any foliage on divided plantlets to approximately 2–4 in. above the water line, then pot the young plants into aquatic compost or suitable garden soil in containers or planting beds. Pieces of rhizome are pushed into the compost, then covered with a shallow layer of gravel or pebbles.

Water lilies Water lilies are also propagated by cutting the thick rootstocks so the divided young portions contain an "eye," or growing point. After removing the old crown or rootstock, cut off pieces of the outer or younger roots, approximately 6 in. long. After trimming off the thin, fibrous roots to within 3/4–1 1/4 in. of the rhizome, partially bury these pieces in containers of aquatic compost or suitable garden soil. Cover with pea gravel; then submerse it in shallow water so that the growing point is no deeper than 4–6 in.

Seed

Many marginal and deep-water aquatics can be grown from seed, which produces large numbers of offspring. After collection, store the ripe seeds in jars of moist moss or distilled water if the seed is not to be sown immediately. To sow, sprinkle the seeds evenly on the surface of firmed aquatic compost in seed pans or half-pots and cover them with a light dressing of fine grit before immersing them in a plastic bowl where the seed pan is just covered with water. Keep the seed pan in full light at around 64°F until germination. As the seedlings grow, gradually increase the water level until they are large enough to be transferred to individual pots, kept submerged in shallow water in a bowl or aquarium just covering the seedlings' growing point. After a further period of growth, the plants will be ready for transferring to their permanent planting areas. The whole process from sowing seed to planting out takes from 18 to 24 months.

One species of water lily, *Nymphaea tetragona* 'Alba,' fails to produce eyes and must be propagated by seed. The seed, which is contained in a jelly-like tissue, is not separated before sowing; it is spread and lightly covered with compost while still intact.

Softwood cuttings

Most submerged oxygenating plants and certain creeping marginals are propagated by softwood stem cuttings taken in spring or early summer. Pinch off young shoots, about 6 in. long, from the parent plant, and bunch six to nine of them together at the base before inserting them into aquatic containers filled with suitable garden soil. The cuttings must remain submerged at all times and kept in full light, until they become established.

Runners and turions

Many of the surface-floating plants spread by means of floating stolons, or runners. Propagation involves simply removing or snapping off the young offshoots and allowing them to grow on separately.

Turions are the swollen buds produced by a limited number of water plants such as frogbit (*Hydrocharis morsus-ranae*) and water violet (*Hottonia palustris*), which over-winter in the mud at the pool bottom. Taken in the autumn, these buds can be stored in a frost-free place underwater and collected as they start into new growth and float to the surface.

Menyanthes trifoliata
The dainty, fringed flowers of this beautiful aquatic attracted several famous herbalists and botanists. The 18th-century botanist William Curtis praised the virtues of the marsh trefoil, or bog bean, for costing nothing and being cultivated without trouble. Earlier, in the 16th century, the well-known herbalist John Gerard described the feather-like flowers as "Dasht over slightly with a wash of light carnation." The healing properties of bog bean are well documented as an infusion against colds.

Stocking the pool

A pool becomes home to a wide variety of plants and animals which can live in harmony when stocking levels are balanced and controlled. Amphibians like frogs and toads, such as the natterjack toad seen here, are attracted to garden pools and, once a local community is established, can become a great ally to the gardener in devouring young slugs and snails. Amphibians should not be removed from one environment to another unless their original home is seriously threatened.

Fish should not be introduced to a new pool until the plant life in it has become established, which takes a minimum of two or three weeks in high summer. It is important to allow stocks of natural foods to build up in the water rather than supply packeted fish food. Additionally, in a pool well stocked with submerged plants, fish waste provides an excellent plant food, and mosquito larvae will stand little chance of survival where surface-swimming fish like orfe are present.

The stocking levels of fish and the choice of species are important considerations if the delicate balance of a clear pool is to be maintained. If fish are the main reason for having a pool, the design may necessitate a pool devoid of plants with filtration systems installed to maintain water clarity and fish health (see page 48). But in most cases a satisfactory harmony can be achieved when the quantity and size of fish are limited. A general guideline to stocking levels is 2 in. of body length to every square foot of surface area. The surface area rather than the pool's volume is the important factor governing stocking levels. This is because the surface area determines the amount of atmospheric oxygen which the pool can absorb. At night the oxygenating plants give out carbon dioxide and deny the pool oxygen, which is why warm, sultry summer nights are a critical time for fish (see below).

When introducing fish in smaller pools, it is better to have several small fish than the same equivalent of body length in large specimens. The big fish are able to devour larger sources of food than smaller fish and this may be at the expense of a mixed population of submerged wildlife. Large specimens of hungry fish can soon create an almost sterile pool with a limited variety of wildlife, which would make the fish depend increasingly on supplies of store-bought fish food. Although hand-feeding has great appeal, dried fish foods are less healthful than the natural supply in a well-balanced food chain. Too much artificial food is often followed by a rise in nitrate levels and the resurgence of algae growth.

Introducing fish

As many ornamental fish are imported, they should be purchased only from reputable sources with quarantine facilities, to ensure that stress-associated diseases and weaknesses are minimized. When choosing, always reject fish with damaged scales or weak, limp fins. Keep further stress to a minimum by transporting them in a darkened box containing a small volume of water in an oxygen-enriched polyethylene bag: this is filled with pure oxygen from compressed cylinders at the fish suppliers, then sealed with an elastic band for the journey. The box should be kept in the car trunk and never exposed to strong sunshine through a car window.

Before introducing the fish into the pool, float the bag on the water surface for a hour to allow the water temperature in the bag to adjust to that of the pond. After this period of acclimatization, release the fish by allowing the pool water to enter the bag slowly, enabling the fish to swim out.

Although aquatic centers may sell other forms of animal life, like snails, which, it is claimed, clean the pond, there is little justification for their inclusion. The ordinary pond snail establishes itself readily, often to the point of excess. The most healthful situation for the development of wildlife is for it to be attracted there naturally, after which it is more likely to establish and breed.

Fish for the ornamental pool

Certain species of fish are more suitable than others for life in a mixed ornamental pool. The right choice of species is as important as the introduction of the appropriate size of fish and the maintenance of correct stocking levels. The wrong choice may lead to damaged plants in constantly cloudy water with very little likelihood of ever seeing the fish. Mixing the species of fish is beneficial, creating a community with different needs that is less at risk from acute food shortages. The main hardy ornamental fish available from commercial sources are described below and some are illustrated, right.

Goldfish The goldfish is a much underestimated fish in terms of its adaptability to a wide variety of situations, and its ability to breed easily in temperate pools, producing interesting color variants and shapes. Its value as an ornamental fish was recognized in ancient China, but only as recently as the 18th century were goldfish bred in earnest in Japan, where most of the modern variants originate. Having a lifespan of 20 years, goldfish can grow to a length of 14 in.; they are tolerant of low temperatures and a wide variety of pH levels, from as low as 5.5 to as high as 9. Taken overall, they are the easiest fish to keep in temperate pools, seldom outgrowing their environment.

Several interesting variants have emerged, one of the most elegant being the comet goldfish with its long, streamlined fins and tail which make it one of the most graceful swimmers in the ornamental-fish community. It is just as hardy and capable of breeding in temperate pools as the common goldfish. Shubunkins are descendants of the common goldfish and are equally hardy. They are valued mainly for their coloring, which ranges from the more common red to blue, brown, black and white; the blue forms are particularly valuable. The Japanese developed the breed during this century. Calico fantails and Japanese fantails are similar to comet goldfish but have more rounded bodies and even larger double tails. The Calico fantail is a multicolored fish with patches of black, red, blue, white, and gold. The Japanese fantail has golden-orange scales with black and white

splashes. They are not as hardy as comets and shubunkins but they always attract a lot of interest due to their attractive coloring and their sedate swimming manner.

Orfe The sleek lines of this elegant fish darting just under the water surface makes orfe one of the most successful ornamental-pool fish, particularly where there is enough room for them to exhibit their speed. It is a European fish, originating in southern Germany, which is hardy but less tolerant of low oxygen levels and pollution than goldfish. The golden orfe is a golden-yellow color on the top, with a silvery sheen underneath. There is a completely silver form too. Orfe are particularly valuable for eating mosquito larvae, and in large pools the striking sight of a shoal of orfe speeding through the shallow water is unforgettable.

Carp The ornamental carp, also known by its Japanese name, koi, has caught the imagination of many pool owners during the latter part of this century. Most aquatic centers tantalize potential customers with displays of huge, beautifully colored carp in crystal-clear water. There is, however, behind the scenes the necessity for a large pump, a filtration system and complex pipework. A pool for carp should be carefully designed and managed and this fish should not be the first choice in a pool where planting is the priority. Although plants can exist in the same pool as large carp, the plants should be protected by covering their roots and any planting area with heavy cobble stones which prevent the inquisitive fish from uprooting the plants and constantly disturbing the soil. An alternative to protecting the roots of water lilies in carp pools is to raise the level of the planting crate or raised planting bed to just below that of the water surface. As carp are natural bottom-feeders they prefer not to spend time very near the surface searching for food.

Carp should be introduced to plant-dominated pools when the fish are small so that they grow up in association with the plants. The carp's rate of growth continues even in modest pools. As they can grow as much as 1 in. in a month in warm water, they should never be introduced to very small pools.

SIX ORNAMENTAL FISH

Comet goldfish

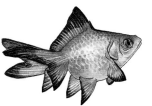

Japanese fantail

Calico fantail

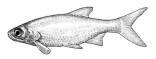

Golden orfe

Carp or koi

RIGHT *The fish population enjoy the oxygenated water from the waterfall. A balance of oxygenators and shade is provided by the water lilies and the water milfoil (Myriophyllum aquaticum).*

Fish for the wildlife pool

The introduction of fish into a wildlife pond requires care if a healthy community of micro-organisms is to be maintained. As large fish devour most of the invertebrates, only a few small species should be introduced which will not grow out of scale with the pool. Exotic-looking fish may appear out of place in a wildlife pool. Some suggested species are:

Rudd Similar in shape to the common goldfish and easily confused with roach, rudd grow to between 3 and 10 in. long. Native to slow-moving or still water, these mid- to surface-water swimming fish have difficulty feeding off the bottom because of their upturned mouths and they tend to feed off plant debris and small insects instead. The golden rudd, which appears more bronze-colored, is a more striking form. Rudd, with their red fins, are a lively addition for a medium-sized to large pond.

Common carp A long-lived fish which, since Roman times, has been grown for its excellent flesh. It is only suitable for large lakes, since its constant foraging on the bottom produces cloudy water.

Green tench This heavy and thick-set, bottom-dwelling fish is seldom seen. It is dark bronze-green above, with a yellow sheen below; its scales are deeply embedded in a thick, slimy skin. A slow-growing fish which can ultimately reach 28 in., it is able to tolerate poorly oxygenated water. A golden form has brighter, orangy colorations.

Trout These fish are only suited to large lakes or pools supplied with cool running water from naturally fed streams or springs, with adequate supplies of oxygen and cool water. Various forms, such as brook trout, brown trout and rainbow trout, each have different levels of tolerance to water temperature.

Minnow These attractive small fish are variable in color, with dark spots or bands on the back and sides. They grow to about 3 in., seldom living longer than five years. Minnows are at home in shallow, moving, clear water on a gravelly bed.

LOOKING AFTER THE POOL

Water gardens need not be especially time-consuming, provided you have given careful consideration at the outset to good design and sound construction. Keeping the water and its occupants in pristine condition requires a certain amount of attention throughout the year, however, as does the prevention of pests and diseases. It is particularly important to recognize and treat problems in a pool at an early stage as the use of chemical sprays has to be severely restricted due to the sensitivity of fish and other water life.

Water in pristine condition brings luxuriant growth and color in high summer. The huge round leaves of Gunnera manicata *(right) provide a cool background to the strong sword-shaped leaves of flag iris* (Iris pseudacorus) *and make the perfect backcloth to the frothy powder-pink flowers of astilbes. The shapely weeping pear by the pool's edge casts interesting shadows in the water, with its delicate gray foliage.*

Keeping the pool water clear

Leaves falling into a small pool can be a major source of pollution. Netting, in addition to acting as a deterrent to herons, can protect the pool from autumn leaf fall. In this pool the netting is sufficiently camouflaged by the pool's raised surrounds not to spoil the contribution this water feature makes to the garden.

As we have seen throughout the previous chapters, good design and planting are of paramount importance in creating conditions which encourage clear water. Cloudy or green water is the scourge of ornamental pools, and particularly of small, preformed pools. The long-term management of a pool involves keeping a watchful eye on the submerged growth of oxygenators and surface leaf cover to see that the right balance of competition for light and food is maintained against the offending algae. If there is too much leaf growth, the pond becomes a tangled mess of oxygenator and water lily leaves; if there is too little, the water may turn green, particularly during prolonged sunny spells.

Clouding of the water, as opposed to greening, can be caused either by fish disturbing any soil on the bottom, or by various forms of water pollution. Soil disturbance by fish may be cured by stocking the pool with only surface-swimming fish (see page 86) or by cleaning the pool bottom. A layer of cobbles in planting crates prevents bottom-dwelling fish from

stirring up the soil in them. Water pollution may be caused inside the pond by the decomposition of animal or plant tissue, in which case you will need to undertake a complete clean-out or partial water change (see page 98). Pollution may be caused externally by dissolved salts in the surrounding soil seeping into the pool. In this case you may need to regrade any slope into the pool or provide a drain to intercept the water; you should at least avoid fertilizing the surrounding area or use slow-release granules which relinquish only a portion of dissolved plant food over a long period.

More often, however, the clouding is caused by algae and, even in the best-managed ponds, there is a surge of algae growth at particular times of year, such as early spring; but this is a transient condition.

Algae

There are two main types of algae which cause problems to the water gardener: the suspended microscopic algae, which are so small and appear in such quantity that the pool looks green, and the filamentous algae, which join together to form long strands known as blanketweed. The former type prevents water clarity but is of little harm to fish, whereas the blanketweed tends to float in otherwise crystal-clear water, choking up small ponds and limiting fish movement.

While the suspended microscopic algae will eventually be starved out by the competition from the other planting, the blanketweed is extraordinarily persistent. It has the advantage of being solid enough to be removed by hand, but it soon returns and is more of a nuisance. Blanketweed favors clear, shallow water which warms up quickly in spring; it is more prevalent when a pool is frequently topped up with tap water, which is rich in mineral salts. Its control involves increasing the competition for the mineral salts on which it feeds by introducing other submerged planting and removing some of the extensive strands by twirling a forked stick or rake in the weed.

Rainwater is always better than tap water for replenishing pools. The best arrangement for topping up is to have a water barrel which collects rainwater from a drainpipe from the roof and diverts it to the pool. This is particularly good for pools linked to a bog garden, since bog plants lose moisture by transpiration and these pools need frequent topping up. Watercourses incorporating waterfalls and streamside planting are notorious for needing replenishment as a result of both evaporation from the waterfalls and transpiration from the plants.

Sometimes it becomes necessary to use chemicals to control algae but, although most brand-name algicides for blanketweed and green water are effective in the short term, the root cause of the problem is likely to persist beyond the effective life of the algicide and the problem will return. Water which is very acid or very alkaline may cause greening and in such cases you can change the water to a more neutral state by adding chemicals sold for the purpose. This should be done extremely gradually.

REPAIRING LEAKS

Most liners, apart from polyethylene, have repair kits which are easy to use, provided the damaged area is clean and dry.

● If the level of a pool persistently drops and remains at the lower level when the pump is not running, there may be a leak just above the point where the water settles down. Closer examination often reveals a hairline tear which can be sealed with a repair patch.

● If the water level drops only when the pump is running, the leak may occur in the watercourse or waterfall; examine the sides carefully, for the tell-tale wet soil under the surface. If it is difficult to dismantle the waterfall, seal the leak with a sealant or point it with fast-drying mortar.

● Pools installed in soils with a very high water table may result in a liner billowing on the surface. Fit a special valve, from aquatic suppliers, into the bottom of a rubber liner to allow land water to enter the pool bottom and prevent pressure from building up. In summer, when the water table drops, the valve prevents water loss from the pool.

Duckweed and certain types of algae can completely cover a pool's surface if not kept in check. While an adequate quantity of submerged oxygenators and water lilies should keep most suspended microscopic algae in check, duckweed can become a menace if not removed early.

Water plant diseases and disorders

Marginal and moisture-loving plants are generally relatively disease-free, with the exception of mildew. The heavy canopy of surrounding lush foliage and the damp atmosphere at the water's edge make ideal conditions for mildew to flourish, but fortunately it is mainly restricted to marsh marigolds (*Caltha palustris*) in mid- to late summer. Mildew is unlikely to kill the plant and, unless the appearance of the gray coating of mildew on the leaves offends, it can be left alone. If the mildew becomes too obtrusive, you should completely remove the diseased foliage to encourage the rapid growth of fresh young leaves.

Water lilies are the most likely water garden plants to encounter any disease and in most cases this takes the form of leaf spot and, more rarely, root rot. Leaf spot appears as either dark patches on the foliage, which eventually cause the affected areas to rot away, leaving an almost disintegrated leaf, or as dry, brown leaf edges which eventually rot. If fish are present in the pool all you can do is remove affected leaves at the earliest sign of infection. Weak fungicidal sprays can be used in the absence of fish.

A less common, but more serious and debilitating disease is a root-rotting disorder known as crown rot. The early symptoms are yellowing of the leaves, which soon die, with little or no regrowth of clean, healthy pads. If the infected plants are lifted out of the water they will reveal rotting and evil-smelling roots that should be destroyed. If the disease is caught early enough, there is a chance that other plants in the pool will not have become infected, particularly if they are another species or cultivar, but keep a watchful eye for similar symptoms on water lily foliage in the same pool. If all seems clear after a few weeks, the removed plant can be replaced with a new one.

Occasionally marginals suffer from a condition known as reversion. This occurs in plants which have either variegated or unusual-shaped leaves or stems and causes the plant to exhibit a growing number of plain green or normally shaped stems and leaves. Unless these plain leaves or stems are removed as soon as they are noticed, they will eventually take over the plant. Reversion should not be confused with the gradual greening which some variegated marginals like *Iris pseudacorus* 'Variegata' experience as the summer advances. This is a perfectly normal aging process of the leaves.

Reversion is a quite similar disorder to fasciation, which occurs in water lilies and causes them to produce numerous malformed leaves and no flowers. Closer examination of the rootstock reveals a proliferation of curled leaves and stems. Sometimes a few normal leaves are present and can be tried for propagation purposes by removing them from the rootstock with a small piece of the root tissue (see page 86). Neither reversion nor fasciation can be controlled by chemicals but, as these conditions are not transmitted to other plants, they need not be considered serious disorders.

Aquatic pests

Pests are more of a nuisance than diseases in the water garden, particularly on water lilies. The rate of growth in aquatic conditions is so prolific that pest attack seldom kills its host, but it can cause unattractive holes and marks on the leaves. The succulent leaves of aquatics prove a great attraction to aphids, particularly to the water lily aphid, which is prevalent on tissue above the water line. Fish will devour any they can reach and spraying colonies of aphids with a strong jet of water dislodges considerable numbers onto the water surface to provide a good meal for them. Similarly, ladybird larvae devour large numbers of aphids and their introduction makes an excellent form of biological control. These physical and biological methods of control are the only direct means possible where there is a population of fish in the pool. But they can be supported by reducing the numbers of over-wintering aphid eggs. In late summer the water lily aphids leave the pool to over-winter on the stems of neighboring plums and cherries, and if these two species are sprayed with a winter wash to kill the eggs, the life cycle is broken and the population of aphids reduced.

The central foliage of water lilies begins to thrust above the surface of the water when the plant is in need of division. The flowering potential of this beautiful water lily in a Japanese-style garden will soon be seriously impaired if it is not divided and the plant will become increasingly rank in growth, with fewer flowers on the water surface.

Leafhoppers are also attracted to the aerial foliage of water lilies, particularly the crowded leaves of overgrown plants which are thrust above the water. Like aphids, they damage the plant by sucking the sap, and in severe infestations cause the leaves to go brown. They are unlikely to be a problem if all the water lily foliage is floating on the surface of the water and you keep the crowns regularly divided (see page 84) so that the aerial foliage of the water lilies is not allowed to build up significantly.

While aphids and leafhoppers reduce the vigor of water lilies by sucking sap, their presence is not nearly so obvious as the larvae of leaf-biting insects such as moths, which cause unsightly holes and in some cases totally skeletonized leaves. One of the most common pests to destroy foliage is the brown China mark moth, whose larvae eat large holes around the leaf margins. These small moths, about 1 in. long, with irregular white patches on brownish-orange wings, are most commonly seen in the latter part of the summer. Their creamy-colored caterpillars hatch from egg clusters just beneath the surface of the leaf and, after chewing and shredding foliage, protect themselves before they pupate by forming shelters out of cut pieces of foliage which they stick onto the leaf. During the period prior to pupation they are able to move around the edges of water lily leaves in cocoon-like cases, with only their head and forelegs protruding, giving them the common names of "bagman caterpillars" and "sandwich men." Their control consists of removing any seriously affected leaves by hand and netting any pieces of floating foliage which may be acting as homes for the over-wintering pupae. The closely related China mark moth inflicts similar damage by eating into the leaf stems of the water lilies.

This method of providing a portable home or protection by using foliage is perfected by another water lily pest, the caddis fly larva. Its house building takes that of the China mark moth a stage further by strengthening the framework with small sticks, pieces of shell and sand. The adults resemble small brown moths between ¼ and ½ in. long that lay their eggs in long, jelly-like tubes sometimes seen dangling from foliage on or near the water surface. After emerging from the eggs, the larvae form their protective cases and swim around, feeding on any plant tissue they can find, in some cases completely desiccating the water lily leaves. Chemical control is impossible but any fish will normally keep down the population levels.

One of the most disfiguring pests to attack water lily foliage is the leaf-mining midge. Like those of most aquatic pests, their attacks seldom kill the plant but weaken the host and spoil the attractive foliage. After hatching from eggs laid on leaf surfaces, the leaf-mining midge larvae burrow just under the surface, creating a network of disfiguring lines. Eventually the damaged tissue dies away, resulting in large sections of decomposing leaf which can form a skeletonized appearance. The pest can be kept in check by the presence of fish and removing by hand any infected leaves promptly.

A less common grub which can also skeletonize water lily leaves through its voracious eating habits is the water lily beetle. Like the water lily aphid, it over-winters on vegetation beyond the pool, in this case on the dead stems of marginal plants at the poolside. The small brown adult lays clusters of yellow eggs on the surface of water lily leaves. Several generations of the small, brown, slug-shaped larvae join the adults in a gorging session on the foliage before producing their over-wintering stages, which pupate in the surrounding undergrowth. As fish cannot reach the larvae to eat them, jetting the foliage with water is one way to dislodge heavy infestations. Alternatively, if the lily pads are temporarily submerged by raising the water level or placing wire mesh over them, the fish will be able to reach the offending larvae. Cutting down marginal foliage around the pond to almost ground level in the autumn denies a home for over-wintering larvae.

Although it is sometimes sold in conjunction with the more beneficial ramshorn snail, the common pond snail or freshwater whelk is more likely to be a nuisance than a beneficial addition to a pool. The ramshorn snail, which derives its common name from the shape of its shell, confines its diet to algae, unlike the common pond snail with its spirally pointed shell which can turn its attention equally to succulent young water lily pads or other soft aquatic tissue. The jelly-like eggs of the common pond snail can be easily seen on the underside of most water lily leaves, and when the population of adult snails reaches harmful levels, you can use lettuce leaves as bait on the pool surface for 24 hours. The snails are soon attracted to this readily available soft foliage and can then be netted off easily.

LEFT *Caddis fly larvae feed on the foliage of aquatic plants, constructing an elaborate form of protection around their soft bodies to protect them from predators during their year as larvae. The adult flies are like brownish moths and are mainly nocturnal. They are named after the caddis man—an old name for peddler—who decorated his clothes with samples of his wares.*

Fish problems

While ornamental fish are resistant to most serious disorders, problems can occur through overstocking the pool, through pollution or through buying from unhygienic suppliers. Most ornamental fish sold at aquatic centers have been imported and require a quarantine period before being displayed or sold, particularly the highly decorative types which may have already been weakened by inbreeding.

important, both in the quantity and the type of food used. If the only source of fish nourishment is poor-quality dried food, this can lead to physiological disorders of the type common to any organism restricted to an unbalanced diet.

Pollution may also take the form of chlorine pollution, through the addition of large volumes of tap water. Replenishment from the house water supply is most likely to be needed in the summer, and this is the period when tap water is likely to have higher levels of chemicals. The chlorine content of tap water, in addition to the chemical changes caused by other salts contained in it, puts a fish under stress. If you have to use tap water rather than rainwater, you should add a brand-name neutralizing agent for chlorine, one that is available at most good fish stockers or aquatic centers. You should also feed live food to the fish whenever possible.

Their initial introduction to the pond is the first stressful time for fish, particularly if there is little vegetation to hide under when recovering from the trauma of a journey. Having settled into a new community, there is then a strenuous period of activity at spawning time for male and female fish alike. The post-spawning period can find a fish exhausted and especially vulnerable to disease. A severe winter is also weakening, particularly during prolonged frost. If the pool is frozen over for long periods and bubbles of methane gas cannot escape from under the ice, the toxic methane is reabsorbed into the water, further weakening the fish in their torpid state. Any violent shock waves caused by breaking the ice on a pond in winter can be extremely damaging to fish, so you should melt the ice gradually instead (see page 105). Long, hot summer nights are a difficult time, particularly for orfe. Warm water is less able to absorb atmospheric oxygen than cold water, and this factor, coupled with the extra carbon dioxide present during the night from the submerged plants, can cause fish to leap out of the water in desperation for more oxygen. A fountain or waterfall kept running overnight in such conditions is extremely valuable.

Water pollution is one of the greatest enemies of fish. While the species of ornamental fish recommended in the chapter on Planting and Stocking the Pool, pages 86–7, are tolerant of many infections from fungi and bacteria, the gardener may inadvertently cause stress to fish through indirectly related activities near the pool. If you examine the instructions on any chemical weedkillers or garden insecticides and pesticides, they carry a common warning to avoid using near fish. Extreme caution is therefore necessary when using these chemicals in the garden and they should not be applied on windy days or in very wet weather, when heavy surface runoff may leach into the pool, with harmful effects on fish.

Pollution is not always attributable to chemicals, however. Excess fish food will pollute the water when left to decompose, so the feeding regime is

Fish diseases

The diseases mentioned below are not a comprehensive list of fish ailments but a summary of the more likely disorders which you may encounter. Brand-name remedies, available from good aquatic centers or fish stockers, should first be discussed with a fish expert. When removing fish for treatment do not, on any account, handle them but hold them in a soft net while applying localized medicines.

One of the most likely diseases to attack a weak fish is fungus, which produces tufts of cottonlike growths on the body or fins. If caught early, larger fish can be treated with Desa Fin in a separate tank. It is not contagious.

The early stages of fungus should not be confused with white spot, a parasitic disease with tiny, clearly defined white spots occurring on the body and fins, causing the fish to scrape themselves on the bottom in an attempt to stop the itching. It is more likely to occur in warm water and is not generally a problem for cold-water fish, where adequate quarantine was given before introducing them to outside ponds. Although it is possible to treat white spot if caught early, severely infected fish are best destroyed. Control involves removing all the fish from the pool for treatment with a proprietary remedy and leaving the pool devoid of fish for a minimum of a week, when the parasite will die through lack of a host.

Fish scraping against the bottom and sides of a pool to relieve irritation may be the result of one of the many single-celled organisms which cause slime disease. The fish's whole body can eventually be covered in a grayish film and the fish appear listless, with its fins clamped close to its body. Treatment is difficult once the infection is advanced but, if identified early, the fish can be bathed in a solution of fungus eliminator concentrate.

There are many bacterial infections which can cause rotting tails or fins, ulcers, spots and red patches. If these infections appear more frequently than in rare, isolated occurrences, the cause may be pond water which is so dirty and unhygienic that there is a need for a complete clean-out or a partial water change (see page 98). Infected fish should be isolated and treated with brand-name remedies.

Fish pests

There are few ornamental fish ponds that have not been visited at some time by a heron. Once a heron tastes success it will persist until it devours most of the fish, despite any number of protective measures. If the pool is not too big, you might resort to heavy-duty nylon netting, supported by a timber grid. Frustration will eventually cause the heron to lose interest, but only after several attempts at overcoming the netting, either by tearing the nylon with its strong beak or weighing the net down. While the system of strands (see right) and decoy herons are claimed to have some success, it is more a matter of the availability of alternative food sources which govern the likelihood of a visit.

There are many other predators living within the pool. Great diving beetles, dragonfly larvae, water scorpions and water boatmen are all capable of attacking small fish or fish fry and inflicting damage to their scales, which can then become infected. Many predators are difficult to eliminate from a pond, and any efforts to do so must be measured against the minimal occurrence of serious damage.

More damaging and potentially distressing is a smaller pest, the anchor worm. The most likely sources of infection are fish suppliers whose standards of hygiene are insufficient to control outbreaks of the pest in large, mixed-fish communities. The anchor worm has a thin, white, tube-like body and a barbed head which embeds itself in the tissue underneath the fish's scales, causing ulcers or tumor-like growths. The affected fish must be caught and, while being held in the net, the parasites painted with a solution of potassium permanganate. You can also feed the fish with tetra anti-parasitic medicated food, and use parasitic guard concentrate at the recommended dose. The anchor worms can then be removed carefully with a pair of tweezers and the affected areas painted with an antiseptic solution.

Fish lice are flat, jelly-like creatures about ¼ in. long which can be found on fins or gill plates. They are common pool inhabitants, their eggs hatching out at regular intervals from the surfaces of stones or leaves. The treatment is the same as that described for the anchor worm.

Where herons threaten an ornamental fish collection, they may be deterred by the use of inconspicuous horizontal threads placed around the margins, as around this wildlife pool. The heron generally alights a few feet from the pool before slowly stalking to the shallow water. By having the threads at 6 in. and 14 in. above ground level, supported by a series of short bamboo canes, the heron finds it more difficult to move toward the pool without being alarmed.

Cleaning the pool

SIGNS THAT A POOL NEEDS CLEANING OUT

● Water lilies reaching overgrown proportions, with closely packed leaves growing upright and taking up too much space on the water surface. As water lilies need dividing in this condition, it is probably worth cleaning out the whole pond.

● The color of the water may give some clue to its quality. Although green water is a common phenomenon and more likely in a newly constructed pool, dark or black water indicates a buildup of rotting organic matter either from too many leaves having blown into the pond or from submerged oxygenators that have died down and decomposed.

● The buildup of fish waste, resulting from high stocking levels of fish combined with other rotting organic matter, can lead to the accumulation of a thick layer of putrid black sludge on the pool bottom, which releases harmful methane gas and pollutes the water. Occasionally the water may turn a milky color as a result of decay, from a dead fish or creature hidden from view.

There is no hard-and-fast rule on how often a pool should receive a complete clean-out. Many factors determine the need for this, such as the stocking level of fish and plants, the volume of water, the type of planting and the thoroughness with which the pool has been maintained. An unfiltered pool, heavily stocked with fish and submerged plants which have never been cut, may need cleaning out every other year, or no less than once in three years.

Sometimes there are signs within the pool which indicate the need for action, and these are listed, left. All these conditions can be helped by carrying out a partial water change; that is, pumping or siphoning out approximately one-third of the fouled water in spring and autumn and replacing it with clearer water. It is important to do this over a number of changes: if it was undertaken in one operation it could change the water chemistry too quickly, resulting in stress to any fish and the possibility of the green algae building up again.

A complete clean-out is best done between spring and late summer, the earlier in the season the better. An inflatable pool, such as a children's paddling pool, is ideal for temporarily housing the pond's occupants. Fill the holding pool with water from the main pool (to reduce stress to the fish), using a submersible pump; pump out the remaining water into a drain. Keep as much as a third of the original pool water, unless it is seriously polluted, because it is rich in beneficial microscopic life that helps in re-establishment after the clean-out.

It is easier to catch the fish when the water level drops in the main pool, but do not allow this to get too low before using the net as it becomes difficult to see the fish in muddy water. The submersible pump should have a fine strainer on the intake to prevent sucking up small fish and other creatures into the impellers of the pump; keep the pump's strainer or inlet above the bottom sediment to prevent frequent clogging up, and clean the strainer frequently during the emptying process. As the fish are netted out, this provides an excellent opportunity to examine them thoroughly for any signs of parasites or diseases.

Even if the fish seem clear of problems, it is a useful precaution to add a proprietary sterilant or antiseptic to the holding pool in case the fish are accidentally damaged in the transfer from the main pond.

The marginal plants will survive for a day or two without being submerged in water, but the oxygenators must be temporarily submerged in large buckets or plastic trash cans of clean water once the water level drops to expose their foliage. If the oxygenators are containerized, it is better to make bunches of young stems for replanting into fresh soil in the containers rather than keep the original soil and roots in the planting crates. Oxygenators soon desiccate when exposed to air and it is vital to their survival to transfer them speedily to temporary quarters.

Once the fish and oxygenators are removed, the deep-water plants such as water lilies will need protecting from any sunlight or wind by covering their leaves with wet newspaper. Remove them from their containers and replant young shoots, about 6–10 in. long, into fresh soil in the containers as described on page 76. If they are not likely to be returned to the pond within a day or two, they should be temporarily submerged in either the holding pool or another tank.

Once all the plants and livestock have been removed, you can scoop the bottom mud into buckets and dispose of it, keeping a watchful eye for creatures like newts and frogs which bury themselves at the bottom. (This mud is of no value as a top-dressing or addition to the compost heap.) Do not use sharp-edged tools to remove the mud as these could damage the liner; soft handbrushes with plastic dustpans make useful scoops.

Marginal plants which have become rootbound in the aquatic planting crates should be divided before being returned to the pond (see page 84), and the outer portions of the plants inserted into fresh store-bought aquatic compost or suitable garden soil in the containers. If there is no apparent presence of fibrous roots and stems which look easy to split, it will be better simply to pot any rootbound plants into larger containers.

In pools which have permanently submerged planting beds the plants and soil will have to be removed from the beds—an operation which takes considerably longer than removing containers. Discard the old soil in the planting beds, since it has no value in the garden, and refill the beds with fresh aquatic compost. Tease apart the root systems of the different species, then replant, after dividing any overgrown roots. The shoots of the submerged oxygenating plants should be bunched together and then replanted in new compost in the same way as described above, for oxygenating plants in containers (see page 98).

Refill the pool as soon as possible after thoroughly hosing it down and baling out any remaining muddy water. The water in the holding pool can be reintroduced provided it constitutes no more than a third of the pool's total volume. This allows the microscopic creatures to be returned to the main pool to bring immediate life to the sterile tap water. Reintroduce the plants to the water before introducing the fish in order to give the nervous fish some cover. Allow a minimum of a day to elapse to let the temperature of the fresh tap water warm up a little before the fish are finally returned to the pool.

Wildlife pools are seldom cleaned out unless a serious pollution problem occurs, as too many minute creatures are likely to be killed in the process. If the level of mud builds up too much, remove it in stages, preferably in late summer, to cause minimal disturbance to breeding. Sift through the mud carefully before discarding it, in order to retrieve as much visible wildlife as possible and return any creatures immediately to the pond.

A formal reflective pool requires the plants to be in peak condition and occupying the correct proportion of the pool surface. In this pool the water lilies and marginal irises are reaching the size where they would benefit from being divided. Such an operation provides an excellent opportunity to give the pool a complete clean-out.

99

THROUGH THE SEASONS

Water heightens the awareness of seasonal changes by highlighting both the moods of weather and the flowers and foliage of marginal plants. The water surface, busy with life and color in the summer months, becomes a clear mirror to the sky in its winter mode. The husbandry of a caring water gardener will be appreciated in all seasons. Plants that are pampered, fed and protected will reward the gardener by healthy growth and better blooms; fish and animals in and around the pool require diligent precautions against predators. A well-kept pool will always fascinate, all year round.

The uncluttered water surface of this pool seen in late autumn reflects bare stems and russet tints against a clear blue sky. The hoar frost on the shrubs and herbaceous plants in the foreground accentuates their contrasting shapes and habits of growth.

101

Spring

In the early days of spring the bright, shiny flowers of the white marsh marigold *(Caltha palustris alba)* provide a welcome change from the subdued colors of winter. They pave the way for a cheerful display of the more common yellow marsh marigold, which flowers throughout most of the spring. Many dwarf bulbs flower prolifically in the moist soil near water, particularly *Chionodoxa* and *Scilla*, whose rich blues make a vivid contrast to marsh marigolds. As the garden snowdrops *(Galanthus nivalis)* give way to crocuses and daffodils *(Narcissus species)*, the snowflake *(Leucojum vernum)* flowers, resembling giant snowdrops, open their nodding heads of green and white above strong clumps of deep green foliage.

The pool water is normally very clear in early spring, having been well topped off with winter rain. Its crystal clarity enables the green sword-like tips of iris to be clearly seen in the shallow water, piercing the tattered brown leaves of the previous year. Suddenly, the lengthening days are celebrated by a dramatic invasion of frogs, which abandon their usual shyness in the turmoil of their frenzied mating in the shallow water. Their departure is as sudden as their arrival, leaving the familiar spawn suspended beneath a calm water surface. The activity of frogs marks a gentle awakening in the water garden. The fish become more active and begin to explore for food in the shallows.

Many of the marginals start into life now; the variegated manna grass *(Glyceria maxima* var. *variegata)* displays exquisite shades of pink and cream on the tips of the new foliage and, later, the variegated form of the flag iris *(Iris pseudacorus* 'Variegata') sports a display of outstanding creamy-striped leaves. Plants which will often spend the summer unnoticed once they are surrounded by more robust neighbors enjoy the brief lack of competition for the brighter light

The sound of a small trickling stream, and the primroses and ferns at its sides, lift the spirits along a pathway in spring.

of spring. The cuckoo flower or lady's smock *(Cardamine pratensis)*, whose rosy-lilac flowers coincide with the song of the cuckoo, enjoys the moist soil near the water's edge.

One of the most distinctive and unusual spring flowers belongs to the skunk cabbage *(Lysichiton americanus)*, whose intriguing yellow or white arum-like flowers open before the growth of its impressive thick and leathery paddle-shaped leaves, which grow up to 3 ft. high. Similarly, the fascinating flowers of the umbrella plant *(Darmera peltata)* open in soft pink umbels on tall, slender, hairy stems which grow from the fleshy surface rhizomes before the umbrella-like leaves appear.

Spring in the water garden would be incomplete without the primulas, heralding the warmer days with the deep rose-pink flowers of the dwarf *Primula rosea* and the globe-like flowers in shades of lilac, reddish-purple and white of the drumhead primulas *(P. denticulata)*, held just above ground level on thick

stems. The later-flowering candelabra primulas provide an unforgettable fanfare for early summer, when their colors are massed together.

● The latter part of spring is an excellent time to plant aquatics and moisture-loving plants, either in planting crates or permanent beds (see page 46) and to divide and replant any overgrown marginals (see page 84).

● Frost-tender plants which have been overwintered under cover can be returned outdoors; some of them, like the late-flowering *Lobelia cardinalis*, will have produced young growth which can be used as softwood stem cuttings for propagation (see page 84).

● As the young buds begin to break on the colored stems of dogwoods *(Cornus species)* and willows *(Salix species)*, the stems are cut back to within 2–3 in. of ground level to encourage the production of strong young growth which will form next winter's color. If the prunings are cut up into hardwood cuttings 7–9 in. long, and inserted to two-thirds of their length in the moist soil at the waterside, they will root and create new shrubs.

● The moisture-loving beds should be given a thorough weeding and forking over.

● If there is any suspicion of pollution through the accumulation of organic matter on the pool bottom, one-third of the pool's volume should be replaced by fresh water. If the pool has been neglected for several years and a thick layer of sludge has formed on the bottom, this is the best time to clear out the pool (see page 98).

● Although the fish become more active and hungry as spring advances, feeding should be kept to a minimum in the early-spring and you should gradually build up the quantity given as the water temperature increases. Fish food should not be seen floating on the surface for longer than three to five minutes after feeding. Live food such as *Daphnia* or chopped worms will be particularly beneficial at this time.

- The young shoots of *Gunnera manicata* are vulnerable to frost and should be covered by leaves or straw until the risk of frosts is over.
- Scrambling waterside plants like brooklime (*Veronica beccabunga*) or water forget-me-not (*Myosotis* species) should be planted now to soften any exposed bare edges to the pond.
- If the pump was removed for servicing over the winter it should now be reconnected.
- As surface leaves develop, any pipes placed on the pool bottom in the autumn to protect the fish against predators can now be removed.
- Any over-wintered floating plants such as frogbit (*Hydrocharis morsus-ranae*) or fairy moss (*Azolla caroliniana*) can be returned to the pond as soon as the danger of frost has passed.
- Any protective netting or other winter protection can now be removed.

Summer

In early summer the flowers and foliage of the globe flowers (*Trollius* species) make a welcome contrast to the strong upright foliage of the marginals, especially when planted in association with the blue and mauve shades of *Iris ensata* and *I. sibirica*. The globe flowers, with their large buttercup-like flowers in shades of yellow and orange, like the moist soil of the water's edge but should never be waterlogged. The moisture-loving beds should be at their peak now, particularly where there are drifts of astilbes and day lilies (*Hemerocallis* cultivars).

Once the main spurt of early summer growth is over, the pool takes on a tranquil appearance as more flowers open on the water lilies. Toward the end of summer the flowers of the waterside lobelias appear. Although there is slight variation in the leaf characteristics of the species, they all contribute striking crimson flowers, best seen reflected against a dark background. They blend well with the pale blue flowers of pickerel weed (*Pontederia cordata*).

Luxuriant summer foliage and flowers are seen in the day lilies, hostas, astilbes and Himalayan cowslips at the pool edge.

- Deep-water plants should be fed at three-week intervals in summer by pressing brand-name sachets of slow-release fertilizer into the soil close to their roots.
- Remove old water lily flowers regularly throughout the summer and cut back oxygenating plants from time to time to keep them in check. The young growth removed from the submerged oxygenating plants makes ideal material for bunches of new cuttings if more stock is required for the pool.
- Summer is still a good time to divide plants which have become overgrown or which are needed for propagation. There are several floating and shallow-water plants, like water fringe (*Nymphoides peltata*), which are increased by simply separating the runners or plantlets from the parent plant.
- Seedpods can be collected from aquatics at the end of their flowering; the seed is best sown fresh for most species, particularly the moisture-lovers like primulas. Seed from the deep-water plants such as water lilies, water hawthorn (*Aponogeton distachyos*) and golden club (*Orontium aquaticum*) are sown thinly in seed pans or half pots of firmed aquatic compost (see under Propagation on page 84).
- In very hot weather a fountain or waterfall should be kept running throughout the night if fish are present, as it can be a period of severe oxygen shortage. The hotter the weather, the more difficult it is for atmospheric oxygen to be absorbed by the water and any form of disturbance to the water surface, like the vigorous spray from a garden hose, will help to increase oxygen levels in the pool.
- Topping off the water level of a pond is often necessary in long periods of dry, hot weather. Ideally this is best done with tap water stored in rainwater butts around the garden, as this is less likely to upset the chemistry of the pool and result in a fresh surge of algae growth. Water from the house supply is likely to have a higher chemical content in the summer and excessive topping up will invariably lead to green water a few days later.
- Where house tap water is the only source to restore depleted supplies in a pool, introduce it in small quantities daily, rather than all at once, or the change will have a marked effect on both the water temperature and the well-being of the fish.
- Fish will be at their most active on warm days and will be particularly hungry. Supplementary feeding with vitamin-enriched floating pellets helps the fish to build up reserves in winter. Any floating, uneaten food is useful as a guideline to the quantity required. Feeding is best undertaken little and often, and fish soon get into a routine and will readily appear at regular feeding times. *Daphnia* (water fleas) is useful live food where it can be obtained, and certain suppliers have excellent sources of quick-frozen live food which, after thawing, provides a welcome addition to the fish's diet.

Autumn

The subdued light of autumn enhances the subtle shades of foliage around the water garden, particularly the fronds of the moisture-loving ferns such as the royal fern *(Osmunda regalis)*. The pale green colors of the royal fern, which have been such a cool contribution to the pool since spring, now change to delightful golden browns as the fronds respond to the cooler nights. The water hawthorn *(Aponogeton distachyos)* produces a second flush of white flowers which are particularly striking on the water surface in the softer light, as are the heavily scented, creamy-white spikes of bugbane *(Cimicifuga racemosa)* held on stems 4–5 ft. high in the moist bed at the poolside.

The pool surface continues to be a source of fascination as the winter advances, despite the decline of the water lily leaves. The tiny leaves of the floating fairy moss *(Azolla caroliniana)* turn an unusual shade of pink, supporting jewel-like drops of moisture which cling to the leaves before the plants sink to the bottom for winter as the severe frosts arrive. Parrot's feather *(Myriophyllum aquaticum)* seizes the chance to scramble across the relatively empty water surface, displaying its graceful feathery leaves against the dark background.

• If the pool is large enough to allow boots to be worn, the yellowing foliage and spent flowers of water lilies should be cut off to prevent them from rotting in the water.
• If there have been serious attacks of water lily beetle during the previous summer, cut the dying foliage of the marginals hard back to remove the over-wintering home for the beetles.
• Where there is a heavy overhang of leaves which fall directly into the pond, it is worth covering the surface of small to medium-sized pools with rot-proof netting; secure it by pegs around the sides to hold it taut.

A wildlife pool in autumn reflects the tints of the wayfaring tree (Viburnum opulus) *in the foreground.*

• If leaves tend to blow onto the pond, a netting fence can be temporarily secured by canes at regular intervals around the pool perimeter.
• The first frosts will blacken the leaves of *Gunnera manicata*; these can be cut off and draped over the crown for winter protection.
• If the autumn temperatures fall slowly, continue feeding fish with small amounts to build up their strength for winter until they show no further interest.
• The rampant and succulent growth of oxygenators such as Canadian pondweed *(Elodea canadensis)* and curled pondweed *(Potamogeton crispus)* may well have dominated a large area of the water volume by autumn. As severe winters can cause their sappy foliage to rot in the water, excessive growth should now be cut back severely. There is less need for oxygenating plants in the colder, duller days ahead, and rotting foliage gives off harmful methane gas and allows the layer of black sludge on the pool bottom to build up.

• Once the foliage of water lilies and oxygenators has gone, lay open-ended lengths of pipe, 6 in. in diameter and about 18 in. long, on the pool bottom to act as protection for the fish against herons.
• Plant dwarf bulbs into the moist soil surrounding the marginals and moisture-lovers, particularly blue-flowered species, which provide an excellent contrast to marsh marigolds.
• Early autumn is a good time to divide any large marsh marigolds, hostas and astilbes (see page 84), giving the young plants time to establish and make a good display next year.
• Floating plants will need to be lifted and over-wintered in a frost-free greenhouse or on a windowsill in a shallow saucer of water with soil on the bottom. The slightly tender lobelias should be lifted and potted before over-wintering them in a cold frame, with straw or leaf mold covering the pots.
• To ensure their survival, the swollen over-wintering buds of the frogbit *(Hydrocharis morsus-ranae)* should be collected and stored in a safe, frost-free place in a submerged seed tray containing loam and covered with 3–6 in. of water. When these float to the surface the following spring, pot them into small containers of loam and stand them in trays of shallow water in as much daylight as possible for three to four weeks before planting them into the shallow pool margins.
• If a submersible pump is not going to be used during the winter, it should now be removed and serviced. The waterproof electrical connection for the pump can now be used for a water heater, surrounded by a polystyrene collar, which floats on the pool. This is a good time to purchase a heater in readiness for cold days ahead. It could be connected now and left to float in the water ready for turning on at the power switch as soon as the water surface freezes over. Water heaters are relatively cheap and make sensible use of electricity in winter.

Winter

The relative starkness of the garden scene in winter highlights the value of water's impact on it. The reflective qualities of water are at their best in this season, enhancing the silhouettes of trees and the sky on a clear water surface. Many of the birds which seem to have temporarily disappeared during the late summer months reappear to bathe in the pool even on the coldest of days. The wildlife gardener will appreciate the value of having left the dead foliage around the poolside to provide protection for birds during raw winter days.

The shape of trees and the color of their bark are emphasized during this season, particularly the vivid stems of the Westonbirt dogwood (*Cornus alba* 'Westonbirt'), whose fiery-scarlet stems are a cheering sight when caught in the low shafts of winter sun. The dogwoods and willows show their colored stems to best effect when pruned hard in the spring. *Salix alba* 'Chermesina' responds well to hard pruning at the end of winter, which encourages the young orange stems; without hard pruning, this willow would grow into a sizable tree in only a few years.

● Winter interest can also be improved by including one or two evergreens with distinctive leaves in the moisture-loving beds surrounding the pool. A good plant to provide interest in the winter is an evergreen rush (*Carex morrowii* 'Variegata') which forms hummocks of stiff leaves with creamy margins and grows 12–15 in. high. On a larger scale, many of the New Zealand flaxes (*Phormium* species) make interesting, architectural plants with a wide variety of foliage colors, growing to 6½ ft. high. Both of these grass-like plants will survive all but the coldest of winters in a temperate climate, the older specimens generally being particularly hardy.

The dramatic red stems of dogwood (Cornus alba) *and the feathery plumes of pampas grass contribute to the winter waterside.*

● While winter is not the planting time for aquatics and moisture-loving plants, this is an excellent time to plant any surrounding specimen trees or clusters of shrubs. With the clear water surface allowing maximum reflection, containerized woody plants can be moved from place to place to find the best position for reflection. Where currents of cold winds appear to be funneled near the pool, small shelter-belt clusters, or more formal hedges, could be planted to create compartments within the garden, giving further emphasis to the future impact of the pool.

● Make a note of where the winter sunshine stays for longest on the pool surface: this will be helpful for repositioning any weak, submerged plants, particularly the less vigorous water lilies, which could benefit from the extra warmth in the following summer.

● If the plants in raised pools are containerized, protect them from prolonged frost by moving them into warmer quarters inside.

● Raised pools should be protected with boards and matting during severe weather.

● Very severe frosts cause pressure from expanding ice, which can crack raised-pool walls. Electric pool heaters prevent this damage by keeping a small area of the water surface free of ice. This ventilation hole is important in a pool containing fish as it allows harmful methane gas to escape. Placing a hot pan on the ice will achieve the same effect as a water heater and is much better than breaking the ice, which causes damaging shock waves to the fish.

● If freezing weather is likely to persist for a long period, you could lower the level of the water in small ponds fractionally by bailing or pumping out a small amount of water, to create an air gap which acts as an insulation layer in much the same way as double-glazing.

● During unusually mild spells of winter weather, the temptation to feed the fish must be resisted even when they appear to be more active. The body temperature of fish is so low in mid-winter that they are unable to digest dried-food solids adequately.

● The lack of surface and submerged leaves and the clear water associated with winter allows bottom-dwelling and shy fish to be observed more clearly for any signs of infections, particularly fungus, and to take remedial measures.

● Winter is a good time to look critically at the construction detail around the pool edge. Without the heavy growth of aquatic and moisture-loving foliage, rocks and contours can be seen more clearly and any adjustments made where rock movement may have occurred. Improvements in the surrounding gradients or edges to the nearby lawn can be undertaken now without worrying about mowing.

● Water levels may still drop in long, dry winter periods, particularly when there are persistent cold winds. Water butts should be full enough in winter to allow for the replenishment of small pools with rainwater.

105

KEY PLANTS FOR THE WATER GARDEN

The diverse range of plants suitable for a water garden has been grouped together in categories for the deep and shallow water depths of a pool and for the moist and boggy areas surrounding it. Most of the plants listed are hardy and readily available at good aquatic centers. Unlike most other decorative garden perennials, aquatics are best planted in the summer months and will grow quickly in conditions where there is a constant water supply. This rapid growth makes their careful choice particularly important if the water garden is not to become overgrown in a short space of time.

A masterly selection of moisture-loving plants, predominantly astilbes and Hosta sieboldiana, exploits its poolside setting to gain the maximum value from their reflection. Their contrasting outlines and color combination are caught in a shaft of sunlight in a woodland setting. The foliage in the foreground is that of skunk cabbage (Lysichiton).

Water lilies

Hardy water lilies

This selection of hardy water lilies (*Nymphaea* species and hybrids) is grouped into the main color shades. The depth of growing medium required below the growing point in a planting crate for a small to medium-sized pool is 6–9 in. It is difficult to be specific about the surface area each plant will occupy, but in warm water, with ample sun and a rich soil, a plant with little competition can reach three or four times the spread of a plant in a densely populated and shaded pool. The planting depths below refer to the depth of water above the growing point and not the depth of the pool.

Nymphaea *'Pink Sensation'*

(v) vigorous: 15–36 in.
(m) medium: 1–1½ ft.
(s) small: 6–9 in.

White

N. 'Gladstoneana' (v) has exceptionally large, bowl-shaped, scented blooms which grow to 10 in. across and are surrounded by leaves with rippled edges. It is best suited to large pools, flourishing in 4–5 ft. of water.

N. 'Gonnère' (m) is a compact cultivar with double, thick-petaled, peony-shaped flowers and light green foliage.

N. 'Hermine' (m), profuse bloomer with long-petaled, star-shaped flowers held well above the water. Tolerant of competition and a wide variation in water depths, it performs better in shade than many white cultivars.

N. 'Virginia' (m-v) has large, almost double, flowers with yellowish centers and leaves with red undersides.

N. 'Virginalis' (m-v) is distinctive and free-flowering but often slow to establish. This water lily has purple-flushed foliage and slightly incurving, semi-double, broad-petaled flowers which have a faint rosy tinge.

Pink

N. 'Firecrest' (m), one of the best pinks, has highly distinctive flowers with bright orange stamens inside a dish of delightful, pale pink petals.

N. 'Hollandia' (m-v) is strong-growing with large, double, goblet-shaped blooms over a long period, which deepen with age from a delightful pale pink to a deep rose.

N. 'Marliacea Carnea' (m-v) is one of the most popular pinks, suitable for

large pools and deep water. Its light pink flowers appear almost white from a distance and turn cream with age. The leaves change from purple to green.

N. 'Pearl of the Pool' (m) has cup-shaped, double flowers with strong, slender petals and is one of the best pink water lilies. The circular leaves are a coppery shade on the underside.

N. 'Pink Opal' (s-m) is an easily grown cultivar for smaller pools or tubs with delicate, coral pink flowers held above the water surface.

N. 'Pink Sensation' (m-v) is an outstanding, free-flowering, fragrant cultivar whose flowers remain open well into the late afternoon. The long, oval-shaped petals have a silvery pink sheen and are deeper pink toward the center.

N. 'Rose Arey' (m) has elegant, star-shaped, fragrant flowers and narrow, incurving petals. It requires a year or two to reach its full potential.

Red

N. 'Attraction' (v) has deep red petals, frequently tipped with white when established, but the young flowers are pinky white in color.

N. 'Escarboucle' (v), an outstanding red water lily with large, uniformly colored flowers. Fragrant, vermilion-crimson petals pamper yellow-tipped, reddish stamens. The large, coppery leaves turn mid-green with age and can be lifted out of the water by a strong flower bud underneath.

N. 'Froebelii' (m) is an excellent, small-flowered water lily for shallow water or tubs, with profusions of blood-red, tulip-shaped flowers just above the water surface.

N. 'Gloriosa' (m) has exquisite, large, light crimson flowers that are freely produced; they deepen with age and stay open later than most varieties. An excellent alternative to N. 'Escarboucle' if space is limited.

N. 'William Falconer' (m) has cup-shaped, deep red, yellow-centered flowers with orange-red stamens and small, glossy, maroon leaves.

Yellow

N. 'Charlene Strawn' (m-v) has fragrant, star-shaped yellow flowers, with long, pointed petals, held above the surface of the water.

N. 'Sunrise' (m-v) requires as much sun as possible to produce beautiful, almost tropical-looking, large, yellow flowers with narrow, incurving petals. These are held above the water and often reach as much as 10 in. across. The dark green leaves have somewhat reddish undersides.

Copper, orange and changeable colors

N. 'Comanche' (m) has flowers with deep orange stamens and outer petals turning from yellow to coppery red. The scarlet inner petals become pinkish apricot, while the olive-green leaves are purple when young.

N. 'Graziella' (s) is a delightful, free-flowering cultivar, suitable for tubs, with small flowers which change from apricot-yellow to crimson and olive-green leaves with maroon markings.

N. 'Indiana' (s-m) is an outstanding, free-flowering "changeable" with small flowers mutating from orange-yellow to brilliant copper-red and attractive, purple-spotted leaves.

Tropical water lilies

These dramatic-looking, extremely fragrant plants bring romance and glamor to the water garden, and come in a variety of colors. There are also two categories available: night bloomers, which are open from sundown to mid-morning, and day bloomers, which are open from mid-morning through to late afternoon. These water lilies should be planted from April to November in the southern states and southern California and in June in cooler areas. They require a planting depth of 6–18 in. above the rootstock, an organic-rich soil, and regular feeding with a brand-name water lily food every two weeks. The pool or container should have a consistent water temperature of 70°F or higher. They thrive in intense sun but, being frost-tender, are vulnerable to cool spring weather. However, they will bloom well into early autumn or until the first frost.

Night bloomers

N. 'Emily Grant Hutchings' is an excellent bloomer, with bronze foliage and rose-red flowers that often appear in clusters. It has a spread of 6–12 square ft. and requires 4–6 hours of direct sunlight each day.

N. 'H. C. Haarstick' has bronze foliage and large flowers (up to 8–9 in. in diameter), deep red in color and tinged with purple at the base. It has a spread of 12 square ft. or more and needs 5–6 hours of direct sunlight.

N. 'Red Flare' has red-tinged, maroon foliage and spectacular flowers that have dark red petals and deep maroon stamens. It has a spread of 6–12 square ft. and requires 5–6 hours sunlight.

Nymphaea 'Escarboucle'

No plant depicts the ambience of a water garden better than a water lily. Its distinctive leaves produce vital shade and the unique flowers emerge for a brief display, changing each day in shape and in their subtle colorations.

N. 'Missouri' has pure white flowers that grow up to 14 in. in diameter. It requires 5–6 hours of direct sunlight.

Day bloomers
Blue

N. *capensis*, which thrives in ponds from 10 in. to 3 ft. deep, has a spread of 6–12 square ft. and requires 5–6 hours of direct sunlight. It has green-speckled foliage and distinctive periwinkle-blue flowers.

N. colorata is ideal for tubs, needing just 6 in. of water above the rootstock. It tolerates low light levels, requiring only 3–4 hours of direct sunlight. With a spread of 2–4 square ft., it produces abundant blue flowers.

N. colorata 'Blue Beauty' has a spread of 8–12 square ft. and needs 5–6 hours of direct sun. It has speckled foliage and produces profuse fragrant, blue flowers, up to 8–9 in. in diameter.

N. colorata 'Mrs. Martin E. Randig' adapts to any area of water and has a spread of 6–12 square ft. It has deep lavender-blue flowers and viviporous leaves (leaves with small plantlets on the upper surface). It requires 4–6 hours of direct sunlight.

N. 'Panama Pacific' is hardier than most tropicals and has speckled, viviporous foliage and deep plum-blue flowers. With a spread of 6–12 square ft., it requires 4–6 hours sunlight.

White

N. 'Mrs. George H. Pring' has speckled foliage and many fragrant white flowers that last all day and grow up to 12–13 in. in diameter. It needs 4–6 hours of direct sunlight.

N. 'White Delight' has speckled leaves and large, creamy white blossoms. It is ideal for medium-sized pools, having a spread of 6–12 square ft. It requires 6 hours of direct sunlight.

Yellow

N. 'Aviator Pring' has mottled foliage and large, cup-shaped, yellow blooms that are 10 in. in diameter and grow up to 1 ft. above the water surface. It is ideal for medium-sized pools and needs 5–6 hours of full sun each day.

N. 'Yellow Dazzler' has speckled leaves and bright yellow flowers with a diameter of 10 in., which don't open until late in the day. With a spread of 6–12 square ft., this water lily needs 5–6 hours of direct sunlight.

Rose-yellow

N. 'Afterglow' has abundant blooms that are a blend of yellow, pink, and apricot. It has a spread of 6–12 square ft. and needs 5–6 hours of direct sun.

N. 'Albert Greenberg' has strongly mottled foliage and blooms with pink, gold, and orange hues. An adaptable water lily, it is a robust grower whose flowers will survive the first frost. It has a spread of 6–12 square ft. and needs 3–6 hours of direct sunlight.

N. 'Golden West' has mottled foliage and salmon-pink flowers that deepen to an apricot color on opening. With a spread of 6–8 square ft., it requires 5–6 hours of direct sunlight each day.

Lotus

Nelumbo nucifera, the sacred or Egyptian lotus, is a winter-hardy perennial that produces wonderful leaves and heavily fragrant blossoms. There are a variety of colors available, including white, yellow, pink, and rose. These plants require 2–4 in. of still water above the soil level and grow from 1 to 7 ft. above the water surface. Planted in March or April in southern areas and in May or June further north, they take a full year to become established and need an organically rich topsoil. They also need 3–4 weeks of sunny weather, with temperatures of 80°F or higher, and 5–6 hours of sunlight.

N. 'Alba Grandiflora' has large leaves and fragrant, white flowers, 10–11 in. in diameter. It grows to 4–5 ft.

N. 'Chawan Basu' is free-flowering, producing creamy white flowers edged with a delicate pink. Ideal for a tub garden, it grows to 2–3 ft.

N. 'Empress' produces single, pure white flowers edged with deep pink. A vigorous grower, it is pleasingly fragrant, the blooms lasting well when cut. It grows to 3–4 ft.

N. 'Lutea' is the only lotus native to North America and is ideal for pond culture. Its umbrella-shaped leaves can grow up to 2 ft. in width and up to 3 ft. tall. The single, light yellow flowers are 6–8 in. in diameter.

N. 'Momo Botan' has leaves 12–18 in. in diameter and fully double, deep rose flowers with yellow centers. It is excellent in smaller ponds and tubs. It grows to 2–3 ft.

N. 'Mrs. Perry D. Slocum' has large blooms, up to 10 in. in diameter, that change color from deep pink to creamy yellow. This species will make a dramatic contribution to a large earth pond. It grows to 6–7 ft.

N. 'Red Lotus' has deep green foliage and deep rosy red, large-petaled flowers. It is large, growing to 5–6 ft.

N. 'Roseum Plenum' is very free-flowering, with large, double, rosy pink flowers up to 10–12 in. in diameter. It grows to 4 ft.

N. 'Shirokunshi' has tulip-shaped, pure white flowers. A dwarf, growing to only 18 in., it is ideal for small containers or small pools.

N. 'Speciosum' is the classic, single, light pink lotus found in Oriental art. It grows to over 6 ft.

Hardy deep-water aquatics

Aponogeton distachyos
(Water hawthorn)

The double spikes of fragrant white flowers, held just above the water, are 2–3 in. long with contrasting black anthers. The strap-like, floating leaves grow up to 8 in. long and 2–3 in. wide. It enjoys a water depth of between 9 and 30 in., tolerates colder water than water lilies and produces flushes of flower in the spring and autumn.

Golden club
see **Orontium aquaticum**

Hottonia palustris
(Water violet)

This species, ideal for an ornamental pool at a depth of 1½–2 ft., has a crowded spike of delicate, pale lilac or white flowers, 14 in. above the water. Much of the finely divided foliage is submerged and acts as an oxygenator. The plant over-winters in the form of turions (terminal buds) on the pool bottom.

Nuphar
(Yellow pond lily, Spatterdock)

Several species are ideal for still or slow-moving water and conditions which are too deep, shaded or acidic for water lilies. They thrive in water 3–6½ ft. deep and have rough, leathery, oval leaves growing from stout, creeping rootstocks with prominent leaf scars. In some species, these can grow 4 in. thick and up to 6 ft. long. The bowl-shaped, yellow flowers are

held above the water surface. Small species, such as N. *japonica* var. *variegata*, suit shallow ponds or large containers.

Nymphoides peltata
(Water fringe)

A hardy plant for water 6–18 in. deep which spreads rapidly by runners supporting floating, heart-shaped mottled leaves, 2 in. across. The yellow flowers have fringed edges. Too invasive for small pools, it is best suited to large lakes, where deep water restricts it to the shallower sides.

Orontium aquaticum
(Golden club)

The striking white flowers, tipped with yellow, emerge from the water surface like small pokers among the bluish-green, velvety, lance-shaped leaves. These have a bluish sheen on the undersides and can grow to 1½ ft. long but are slightly smaller in water deeper than 1 ft. Golden club is sometimes grown as a marginal.

Ranunculus aquatilis
(Water buttercup, Water crowfoot)

Best suited to large wildlife pools where it can cover the water surface. The charming, small, white, buttercup-like flowers have yellow throats. These are surrounded by small, three-lobed, kidney-shaped floating leaves and finely divided submerged leaves which can grow in water up to 2 ft. deep. It is decorative as well as being a useful oxygenator.

These decorative aquatics grow in the deep zone, adding variety to the water surface.

Spatterdock, yellow pond lily
see **Nuphar**

Water buttercup, Water crowfoot
see **Ranunculus aquatilis**

Water fringe
see **Nymphoides peltata**

Water hawthorn
see **Aponogeton distachyos**

Water violet see **Hottonia palustris**

Aponogeton
distachyos

111

Floating plants

Eichhornia crassipes

Floating plants are an important group, particularly in new pools where they reduce algae and add mystery to the water.

Azolla caroliniana
(Fairy moss)
A fern-like plant whose delicate, lacy, pale green leaves, ½–1 in. across, turn red in the autumn before over-wintering on the pool bottom.

Eichhornia crassipes
(Water hyacinth)
A tropical plant whose rapidly spreading runners can choke up rivers in its native habitat. But in temperate summers the roots make a useful refuge for fish. The unusual foliage is formed from rosettes of shiny and bulbous petioles filled with spongy tissue which support kidney-shaped leaves and spikes of lilac flowers with yellow eyes. In temperate areas it is over-wintered in seed pans in a light, frost-free place on a layer of wet compost.

Fairy moss see *Azolla caroliniana*

Frogbit
see *Hydrocharis morsus-ranae*

Hydrocharis morsus-ranae
(Frogbit)
Resembling a small white water lily, the flowers have three white petals with a yellow center and are surrounded by kidney-shaped, attractively veined, shiny leaves about 1 in. across. It spreads by runners and over-winters by producing turions which, separately on the pool bottom, rise to the surface in spring and grow into new plants.

Ivy-leaved duckweed
see *Lemna trisulca*

Lemna trisulca
(Ivy-leaved duckweed)
Several species of duckweed can be too invasive for an ornamental pool, covering the surface in a green carpet, but this species reproduces more slowly and, if kept under control, can help reduce algae. The light green leaves, just beneath the water surface except at flowering time, are about ½ in. long, each with a single rootlet.

Pistia stratiotes
(Water lettuce)
A rapid rate of reproduction, by stolons, can make this plant a nuisance in tropical waters. The pale green, velvety, wedge-shaped leaves grow to 10 in. long and 4 in. wide. Long roots, white when young, later turn purplish, then indigo, trailing up to 1½ ft. in the water and providing refuge for fish. It should only be planted in outdoor ponds during the summer in temperate areas; it over-winters indoors.

Stratiotes aloides
(Water soldier)
Resembling floating pineapple tops, this unusual plant rises to the surface in the summer to flower and produce several stolons, some of which can over-winter as dormant buds.

Trapa natans
(Water chestnut)
Diamond-shaped leaves with serrated edges form rosettes 2–2½ ft. across which float on spongy, reddish leaf stalks. The hard, black, spiny fruits can be stored in wet moss until the spring.

Water chestnut see *Trapa natans*

Water hyacinth
see *Eichhornia crassipes*

Water lettuce see *Pistia stratiotes*

Water soldier see *Stratiotes aloides*

Oxygenating plants

Callitriche hermaphroditica
(Starwort)

These small slender plants grow in a tight mass and make particularly valuable oxgenators by remaining active in the winter. The light green leaves are ½–¾ in. long, with whorls of stiff, slender, dark green forked leaves which are ⅝–1½ in. long and produce terminal rosettes on thin branching stems.

Ceratophyllum demersum
(Hornwort)

A rootless plant which is useful in shady pools and grows to 1–2 ft. long. It has whorls of stiff, slender, dark green, forked leaves, ⅝–1½ in. long, which crowd toward the apex.

Canadian pondweed
see *Elodea canadensis*

Curled pondweed
see *Potamogeton crispus*

Eleocharis acicularis
(Hair grass)

A variable species which has needle-like, pale green leaves up to 8 in. long and a hair's breadth thick. It forms neat, small, grassy tufts.

Elodea canadensis
(Canadian pondweed)

One of the finest oxygenators for garden ponds, though it can become invasive if not trimmed back. The densely branched stems are covered in permanently attached, curving, mid-green whorls of pointed leaves up to ½ in. long and just under ¼ in. wide.

Fontinalis antipyretica
(Willow moss)

An aquatic moss which grows on boulders and logs. It has branched, triangular stems, 8–20 in. long, bearing olive-green to brown, moss-like leaves ½ in. wide.

Hair grass see *Eleocharis acicularis*

Hornwort
see *Ceratophyllum demersum*

Lagarosiphon major

A very efficient oxygenator, similar to *Elodea*, but with single, dark green, curved-back leaves which are not in whorls but in spirals. The dark green stems can grow to 3 ft. 3 in.

Myriophyllum

Several species act as good oxygenators, producing narrow, bright green, needle-like leaves, 2 in. in length. The leaves are held on long, branching stems, as in M. *verticillatum* (whorled milfoil), or densely packed stems of finely divided foliage, as in M. *aquaticum* (syn. M. *proserpicianoides*), known as parrot's feather, whose soft stems emerge from shallow water, creeping over the edges of pools or tubs, or M. *spicatum*, which has whorls of foliage.

Myriophyllum spicatum

A selection of submerged oxygenators should be planted in new pools, allowing a bunch for every square foot of water surface, to help reduce algae.

Potamogeton crispus
(Curled pondweed)

The stems of this plant can grow to an incredible 13 ft. long. It has narrow, translucent, stalkless leaves which are about 3 in. long and ¼–½ in. wide. They also have seaweed-like, wavy edges.

Starwort see *Callitriche hermaphroditica*

Willow moss
see *Fontinalis antipyretica*

Marginal plants

Lysichiton camtschatcensis

Acorus gramineus
(Japanese rush)

A small, grassy-leaved plant, suitable for stream edges, which carries its pointed leaves in two distinct ranks. 'Variegatus,' a decorative cream-striped form, is also suitable for pools and as a specimen plant for sink gardens.
Size H and S: 8–12 in. **Water depth** 0–3 in. **Flowering season** Grown for foliage. **Planting partners** *Juncus effusus* 'Spiralis,' *Lysimachia nummularia*, *Typha minima*.

Alisma plantago-aquatica
(Water plantain)

This striking plant is excellent for the wildlife pool. It has a rosette of bold, long-stalked, ribbed, ovate leaves, up to 2 ft. long, and rosy-white flowers.
Size H: 1½–2½ ft.; S: 1½ ft. **Water**

depth 0–1 ft. **Flowering season** Mid-summer. **Planting partners** *Butomus umbellatus*, *Pontederia cordata*.

Amphibious bistort
see ***Polygonum amphibium***

Arrow arum
see ***Peltandra sagittifolia***

Arrowhead
see ***Sagittaria sagittifolia***

Arum lily
see ***Zantedeschia aethiopica***

Bogbean see ***Menyanthes trifoliata***

Brooklime see ***Veronica beccabunga***

Bulrush see ***Schoenoplectus lacustris tabernaemontani***

Burr reed see ***Sparganium erectum***

Butomus umbellatus
(Flowering rush)

An elegant plant which thrives in shallow water, with long, thin, dark green, triangular leaves growing up to 3 ft. long and ½ in. wide. The individual umbels of charming, reddish-white flowers are 1½–2 ft. above the leaves. Dividing the rootstock ensures abundant flowers.
Size H: 2–4 ft.; S: 1½ ft. **Water depth** 3–5 in. **Flowering season** Late summer. **Planting partners** *Alisma plantago-aquatica*, *Pontederia cordata*.

Carex
(Sedge)

The long, narrow leaves of sedges make them valuable waterside plants, particularly for informal and wildlife pools. *C. elata* 'Aurea' is a striking yellow-foliaged plant for shallow water with inconspicuous flower spikes.
Size H: 15–24 in.; S: 1 ft. **Water depth** 0–2 in. **Flowering season** Spring. **Planting partners** *Caltha palustris*, *Iris pseudacorus* 'Variegata,' *Peltandra virginica*.

Carex pendula is an elegant plant for the shallow margins of a large pool, with long, grass-like leaves. The flowers form drooping 3 ft. spikes.
Size H: 2–3 ft.; S: 3 ft. **Water depth** 0–4 in. **Flowering season** Early summer. **Planting partners** *Acorus calamus* 'Variegatus,' *Iris pseudacorus*, *Mimulus ringens*.

Cotton grass
see ***Eriophorum angustifolium***

Eriophorum angustifolium
(Cotton grass)

Decorative in flower, this spreading marginal carries tassels of cotton-wool flowers above coarse, grassy foliage.
Size H: 6–12 in.; S: indefinite. **Water depth** 0–2 in. **Flowering season** Mid- to late summer. **Planting partners** *Alisma plantago-aquatica*, *Ranunculus flammula*.

Flowering rush
see ***Butomus umbellatus***

Glyceria maxima
var. *variegata*

A striking variegated grass which should be kept in check in all but extensive plantings. Its green-, white- and cream-striped leaves are tinted with lovely flushes of pink during the spring.
Size H: 2½–3 ft.; S: indefinite. **Water depth** 6–12 in. **Flowering season** Mid-summer onward. **Planting partners** *Calla palustris, Caltha palustris palustris, Menyanthes trifoliata.*

Houttuynia cordata

A rapid-spreading plant for pool edges, growing to 18–20 in., with white flowers and heart-shaped, bluish-green leaves which have a pungent smell when crushed. Double-flowered 'Flore Pleno' is slightly less vigorous than the species. *H. cordata variegata*, also less vigorous, grows to 1–1½ ft. and has vividly colored, variegated leaves in crimson, green and cream shades, intensified by full sun. It should be planted at the water's edge so that the foliage is not submerged.
Size S: indefinite. **Water depth** 0–2 in. **Flowering season** Mid- to late summer. **Planting partners** *Acorus calamus* 'Variegatus,' *Iris laevigata* 'Variegata,' *Ranunculus flammula.*

Iris

There are several species, within this large genus, suitable for both formal and informal waterside plantings. *I. laevigata*, one of the finest marginal irises for shallow or muddy water, has blue flowers on stems about 2 ft. high, emerging from within smooth, sword-shaped leaves. A wide variety of cultivars are available which provide a beautiful range of flower colors. 'Variegata' maintains its striking variegation throughout the summer.
Size H: 2–3 ft.; S: indefinite. **Water depth** 0–4 in. **Flowering season** Early to mid-summer. **Planting partners** *Calla palustris, Myosotis palustris, Veronica beccabunga.*

Iris pseudacorus, a very vigorous, common, yellow-flowered marginal found along riverbanks and streams, needs a large pond to be effective. The strong, stiff, bluish-green, sword-like leaves grow to 3 ft. and are 1 in. wide. There are several cultivars with subtle color shades and the excellent 'Variegata' has striped foliage which turns green as summer progresses.
Size H: 3–4 ft.; S: indefinite. **Water depth** 0–1 ft. **Flowering season** Spring. **Planting partners** *Hypericum elodes, Peltandra undulata, Veronica beccabunga.*

Japanese rush see *Acorus gramineus*

Juncus effusus 'Spiralis'

A curious little marginal plant for the shallow edges of small pools whose dark green, corkscrew- and needle-like stems can straighten easily. These should be removed at once.
Size H and S: 1–1½ ft. **Water depth** 0–2 in. **Flowering season** Grown for foliage. **Planting partners** *Myosotis palustris, Myriophyllum aquaticum, Typha minima.*

Butomus umbellatus

Marginal plants prefer the shallower water at the poolside, providing a wide variety of form, color and texture to both formal and informal planting schemes.

Lizard's tail see *Saururus cernuus*

Lysichiton americanus
(Skunk cabbage)

An impressive plant for the margins of large ponds or streams which produces massive, striking leaves, especially if it is grown in rich, deep soil. Its yellow, aroid-like flowers are susceptible to early frosts. The white *L. camtschatcensis* is less vigorous and blooms slightly later.
Size H: 3–4 ft.; S: 4 ft. **Water depth** 0–4 in. **Flowering season** Spring. **Planting partners** *Menyanthes trifoliata, Iris sibirica, Ranunculus lingua.*

Mentha aquatica
(Water-mint)

A spreading plant, similar to the common culinary mint and a useful colonizer of shallow pool margins. Its pungent-smelling leaves and whorls of lilac flowers should be kept in check. **Size** H: 2–3 ft.; S: indefinite. **Water depth** 0–4 in. Flowering season Mid-summer. **Planting partners** *Houttuynia cordata*, *Iris pseudacorus*, *Pontederia cordata*.

Mimulus guttatus
syn. *M. luteus*

One of the few species suited to the saturated, rather than moist, areas of the pool margins. It has abundant yellow flowers on 1 ft. spikes, hollow stems and soft green, toothed leaves and will readily self-seed in boggy areas. It is a variable species, giving rise to several excellent forms. **Size** H and S: 1–2 ft. **Water depth** 0–2 in. **Flowering season** Mid- to late summer. **Planting partners** *Iris ensata*, *Myosotis scorpioides*, *Veronica beccabunga*.

Myosotis scorpioides
(Water forget-me-not)

A delightful plant for shallow pool edges with semi-prostrate stems and a prolific display of light blue flowers with yellow eyes. There are several attractive variants and forms. **Size** H: 9–12 in.; S: indefinite. **Water depth** 0–4 in. **Flowering season** Summer. **Planting partners** *Glyceria maxima* var. *variegata*, *Pontederia cordata*.

Peltandra sagittifolia
(Arrow arum)

This plant has distinctive, bright green arrow-shaped leaves, which are conspicuously veined, and white, arum-like flowers. The flowers are 3–4 in. across and are followed by clusters of red berries. The less showy *P. undulata* has narrow, greenish flowers and green berries. **Size** H and S: 1½ ft. **Water depth** 0–8 in. **Flowering season** Early summer. **Planting partners** *Acorus calamus* 'Variegatus' and *Iris laevigata* 'Variegata.'

Polygonum amphibium
(Amphibious bistort)

This rapid-spreading marginal should be restricted to large wildlife pools where its attractive little pokers of pink flowers, held above the purplish leaves, float on the water surface. **Size** H: 4 in.; S: indefinite. **Water depth** 0–1½ ft. **Flowering season** Mid- to late summer. **Planting partners** *Acorus calamus*, *Iris pseudacorus*.

Pontederia cordata

A robust, neatly formed plant whose shiny, olive-green leaves with exquisite swirling markings surround spikes of soft blue flowers. *P. lanceolata* has similar flowers but longer, lance-shaped leaves and is more vigorous. **Size** H: 1½–2 ft.; S: 2 ft. **Water depth** 0–6 in. **Flowering season** Late summer. **Planting partners** *Alisma plantago-aquatica*, *Myosotis scorpioides*.

Ranunculus lingua

A vigorous species with golden-yellow, buttercup-like flowers carried on hollow, reddish stems and glossy, heart-shaped leaves. This species and the larger 'Grandiflora' should be grown only in large wildlife pools which suit their rapid-spreading habit. **Size** H: 2–3 ft.; S: indefinite. **Water depth** 0–1 ft. **Flowering season** Early summer. **Planting partners** *Acorus calamus* 'Variegatus,' *Iris pseudacorus*, *Veronica beccabunga*.

Reedmace see *Typha*

Sagittaria sagittifolia
(Arrowhead)

A distinctive plant producing fine, shiny, arrow-shaped leaves and tiered spikes of white-petaled flowers with a purple blotch at the base of the petals. 'Flore Pleno' is double-flowered. **Size** H: 1½ ft.; S: indefinite. **Water depth** 0–1 ft. **Flowering season** Late summer. **Planting partners** *Acorus calamus*, *Eriophorum angustifolium*, *Menyanthes trifoliata*.

Saururus cernuus
(Lizard's tail)

This plant has curious, creamy-white scented flowers on nodding spikes 4–6 in. long in attractive, bright green, heart-shaped foliage. **Size** H: 1–2 ft.; S: 1½ ft. **Water depth** 0–1 ft. **Flowering season** Mid- to late summer. **Planting partners** *Pontederia cordata*, *Sagittaria sagittifolia*.

Schoenoplectus lacustris tabernaemontani
(Bulrush)

A tall plant, suitable for the margins of large wildlife pools, with thin, dark green cylindrical leaves. 'Zebrinus,' one of the variegated forms most suitable for ornamental water gardens, has horizontal cream stripes in the leaves like porcupine quills.

Size H: 4–6 ft.; S: indefinite. **Water depth** 0–1 ft. **Flowering season** Grown for foliage. **Planting partners** *Caltha palustris*, *Lysichiton americanus*, *Ranunculus lingua*.

Sedge see *Carex*

Skunk-cabbage see *Lysichiton americanus*

Sparganium erectum
(Burr reed)

A rampant plant for larger wildlife pools and much liked by waterfowl. Long, sword-like leaves almost hide the spikes of round, green, burr-like female flowers appearing just below the inconspicuous male flowers.

Size H: 3–4 ft.; S: indefinite. **Water depth** 0–1½ ft. **Flowering season** Mid-summer. **Planting partners** *Glyceria maxima variegata*, *Sagittaria sagittifolia*.

Typha
(Reedmace)

Most reedmaces are too vigorous for the decorative pool and should be avoided. The following species can, however, be used in garden pools. *T. angustifolia*, with its narrow, strap-like, gray-green leaves, is more suitable for the large water garden. The familiar, poker-like, brown flower-heads are held above the leaves and male and female flowers are separated on the stem. *T. laxmannii*, with narrow foliage and a slightly dwarf habit is, of all the tall reedmaces, the most suitable for the water garden.

Size H: 4 ft.; S: indefinite. **Water depth** 0–9 in. **Flowering season** Late summer. **Planting partners** *Sagittaria sagittifolia*; with *Typha angustifolia*: *Acorus calamus* 'Variegatus,' *Lysichiton americanus*; with *T. laxmannii*: *Schoenoplectus lacustris*, *Zantedeschia aethiopica*.

T. minima, with its narrow, needle-like leaves and attractive, round, chocolate-brown flower-heads, is the only reedmace suitable for a small pool.

Size H: 1–1½ ft.; S: 1½ ft. **Water depth** 0–4 in. **Flowering season** Late summer. **Planting partners** *Eriophorum angustifolium*, *Juncus effusus* 'Spiralis,' *Myriophyllum aquaticum*.

Veronica beccabunga
(Brooklime)

This scrambling plant, with succulent stems growing to 1 ft., is invaluable for covering unsightly pool edges. The small, white-centered, blue flowers are about 3 in. across.

Size H: 4 in.; S: indefinite. **Water depth** 0–6 in. **Flowering season** Spring/summer. **Planting partners** *Iris laevigata* 'Variegata,' *Peltandra sagittifolia*.

Water forget-me-not see *Myosotis scorpioides*

Pontederia cordata

Water-mint see *Mentha aquatica*

Water plantain see *Alisma plantago-aquatica*

Zantedeschia aethiopica
(Arum lily)

A slightly tender marginal which, if grown in water 1 ft. deep, can survive the winter months, particularly if the smaller 'Crowborough' is used. The species has shiny, dark green, arrow-shaped leaves and the white flower, like the familiar florists' arum lily, is large, fragrant and grows to about 3–10 in. long, with a central yellow poker.

Size H and S: 2–3 ft. **Water depth** 6–12 in. **Flowering season** Late summer. **Planting partners** *Pontederia cordata*, *Saururus cernuus*.

Moisture-loving plants

Gunnera manicata

These herbaceous plants flourish in the moist soil surrounding the edges of the water garden, provided that excess water can drain away and that the roots of the plants are not waterlogged.

Ajuga reptans
(Bugle)

A carpeting plant invaluable for scrambling over the edges of streams and pools. There are many attractive forms of the species, which has blue flowers and dark green leaves, 2–3 in. long.

Size H: 6 in.; S: indefinite. **Aspect** Sun or shade. **Flowering season** Spring. **Planting partners** *Iris ensata, Leucojum aestivum* and *Lysichiton americanus.*

Aruncus dioicus
(Goat's beard)

An elegant specimen for the poolside with spires of creamy-white, feathery flowers above deeply cut leaves. 'Kneiffii,' an interesting dwarf resembling a fern with finely cut leaves, grows to 2½–3 ft.

Size H: 5 ft.; S: 4 ft. **Aspect** Sun or shade. **Flowering season** Late summer. **Planting partners** *Astilboides tabularis, Eupatorium purpureum,* species of *Hosta.*

Astilbe × arendsii

It would be hard to exclude one of the many excellent forms of *Astilbe* hybrids to add color in a partially shaded site. The handsome, deeply cut foliage in varying shades of green and bronze complements a range of flower colors from strong, deep crimson and magenta to delicate pink and white shades. 'Fanal' has plumes of brilliant crimson flowers; 'Irrlicht' has white plumes over dark green, dissected foliage; 'Bressingham Beauty' has feathery, tapering panicles of rich pink flowers over broad, divided toothed leaflets.

Size H: 2½ ft.; S: 1½ ft. **Aspect** Sun or shade. **Flowering season** Mid- to late summer. **Planting partners** *Filipendula ulmaria, Hemerocallis* 'Stafford,' *Ligularia* 'Gregynog Gold.'

Bugbane
see *Cimicifuga racemosa*

Bugle see *Ajuga reptans*

Cardamine pratensis
(Lady's smock, Cuckoo flower)

An excellent plant for wildlife pools with tufts of cress-like foliage and charming rosy lilac flowers. 'Flore Pleno' has double flowers.

Size H: 1–1½ ft.; S: 1 ft. **Aspect** Full sun. **Flowering season** Late spring. **Planting partners** *Ajuga reptans, Alchemilla mollis, Primula polyneura.*

Cimicifuga racemosa
(Bugbane)

Extremely graceful, delicate, scented, creamy-white flowers are produced on tall spikes like cream bottle-brushes with attractively marked, deeply divided, almost ferny leaves. The purple leaves and deep purple stems of 'Purpurea' contrast beautifully with the creamy-white flowers.

Size H: 5–6 ft.; S: 4 ft. **Aspect** Sun. **Flowering season** Late summer. **Planting partners** *Eupatorium purpureum, Lobelia splendens, Senecio smithii.*

Cuckoo flower
see *Cardamine pratensis*

Darmera peltata
syn. *Peltiphyllum peltatum*
(Umbrella plant)

A most distinctive plant producing round, umbrella-like leaves 1–1½ ft. across on single stems. The flowers appear before the leaves on single stems 2 ft. high, from conspicuous rhizomes on the soil surface. It is functional as well as attractive, the extensive surface rhizomes helping to prevent any soil erosion at the poolside.

Size H: 3 ft.; S: 2 ft. **Aspect** Sun. **Flowering season** Early spring for flowers; autumn for foliage. **Planting partners** *Carex elata* 'Aurea,' *Filipendula ulmaria*, *Menyanthes trifoliata*.

Day lily see *Hemerocallis*

Filipendula ulmaria
(Meadowsweet)

This plant has creamy-white, feathery flower spikes above attractive, deeply cut leaves. There is an excellent yellow-foliaged 'Aurea' and a double-flowered 'Flore Pleno.'

Size H: 3–5 ft.; S: 3 ft. **Aspect** Sun. **Flowering season** Mid-summer. **Planting partners** *Astilbe × arendsii*, *Polygonum bistorta*, *Rodgersia podophylla*.

Giant rhubarb see *Rheum*

Goat's beard
see *Aruncus dioicus*

Gunnera manicata

This plant always attracts attention with its spectacular, distinctive and deeply lobed leaves which can reach 5 ft. across and are borne on prickly leaf stalks. The curious flower spike, like a huge green bottle-brush, is tinged with red and grows 1–3 ft. tall.

It needs ample space to display its architectural value and may need to have its roots contained if it is not to shade out other plants that are also growing in the moist bed.

Size H and S: 6½ ft. **Aspect** Sun or part-shade. **Flowering season** Early summer but mainly grown for its architectural foliage. **Planting partners** This dramatic plant is shown to best effect alone.

Hemerocallis
(Day lily)

The attractive, grass-like foliage and liberal display of trumpet-shaped flowers in a variety of shades make day lilies very popular; they are at their best with an ample moisture supply. There are many cultivars, growing between 2–3 ft. tall, but dwarf forms, such as 'Stella d'Oro,' with an abundance of bright yellow bellflowers, grows to no higher than 16 in. In general, the spread for this genus is the same as the height. For the smaller garden there are miniatures, with contrasting eye zones in the flower, such as 'Catherine Woodbery,' which has lavender-pink blossoms, and 'Stafford,' with star-shaped red flowers.

Aspect Sun. **Flowering season** Mid- to late summer. **Planting partners** with *H.* 'Stella d'Oro': *Astilbe* 'Fanal,' *Hosta undulata* 'Variegata,' *Ligularia dentata*; with *H.* 'Catherine Woodbery': *Astilbe* 'Sprite,' *Hosta undulata erromena*, *Primula vialii*; with *H.* 'Stafford': *Lysimachia nummularia* 'Aurea,' *Mimulus guttatus*, *Polygonum bistorta*.

Astilbe 'Fanal'

Hosta
(Plantain lily)

The numerous species and cultivars of this handsome genus offer a variety of colors, shapes and markings in the broad, radical leaves and lend a lushness to any plant mix. The species vary in size from a few inches high to vigorous forms which, in time, make clumps of up to 5 ft. across.

One of the largest cultivars, *H. sieboldiana*, has a height and spread of 2 ft., while *H. undulata* grows to just 1 ft., with a spread of 1½ ft. The flowers, in shades of mauve, violet and white, appear on spikes above the leaves.

Aspect Sun or part-shade. **Flowering season** Mid-summer but grown mainly for its foliage. **Planting partners** with *Hosta sieboldiana*: *Iris ensata*, *Osmunda regalis*, *Phalaris arundinaceae*; with *H. undulata*: *Houttuynia cordata*, *Iris laevigata*, *Lychnis chalcedonica*.

Iris sibirica

Iris

Several species of iris enjoy the moist, but not wet, soil at the water's edge. *Iris ensata* (syn. *I. kaempferi*) is an exotic iris with large, boldly marked, clematis-like flowers in many beautiful shades. The broad, sword-like leaves have a distinct midrib.

Size H: 2½ ft.; S: 1 ft. **Aspect** Sun. **Flowering season** Early to mid-summer. **Planting partners** *Ajuga reptans*, *Hosta sieboldiana*, *Houttuynia cordata*.

Iris sibirica is a graceful plant for moist to boggy conditions with much more slender, grass-like leaves than most other irises and branching heads of blue- or purple-veined flowers.

There are numerous cultivars in a variety of exquisite shades, all with an area of yellow or white veining in the center of the fall petals.

Size H: 2–4 ft.; S: 3 ft. **Aspect** Sun or part-shade. **Flowering season** Early summer. **Planting partners** *Ajuga reptans*, *Lysichiton americanus*, *Primula pulverulenta*.

Lady's smock
see *Cardamine pratensis*

Ligularia

A genus of large-leaved plants which thrive in moist soil. *Ligularia dentata* (syn. *L. clivorum*) is an impressive, vigorous plant with large, leathery, glossy leaves and crowded heads of orange, daisy-like flowers. 'Desdemona' is more compact with heart-shaped, dark brownish leaves which are a rich mahogany underneath and terminal clusters of large, vivid orange flowers.

Size H: 4 ft.; S: 2 ft. **Aspect** Sun or part-shade. **Flowering season** Mid-summer. **Planting partners** *Acorus calamus* 'Variegatus,' *Mimulus guttatus*, *Schoenoplectus lacustris* 'Albescens.'

Ligularia 'Gregynog Gold,' a hybrid with *L. dentata* parentage, produces large, heart-shaped, deep green leaves and spikes of orange flowers.

Size H: 4–6 ft.; S: 3 ft. **Aspect** Sun or part-shade. **Flowering season** Mid- to late summer. **Planting partners** *Lobelia cardinalis*, *Schoenoplectus lacustris* 'Albescens,' *Scrophularia auriculata* 'Variegata.'

Ligularia przewalskii is a most decorative species with deeply cut, round, dark green leaves supported on almost black stems with tall spikes of small, yellow, daisy-like flowers reaching 6 ft. 'The Rocket' has jagged-edged leaves and lemon-yellow flowers.

Size H: 4–6 ft.; S: 3 ft. **Aspect** Full sun. **Flowering season** Late summer. **Planting partners** *Lobelia cardinalis*, *Schoenoplectus lacustris* 'Albescens.'

Lobelia cardinalis

This plant has impressive bright scarlet flower spikes above rosettes of leaves which may vary from fresh green to red-bronze. It is sometimes grown as a marginal in shallow water but is relatively short-lived if treated in this way and should be lifted every autumn to over-winter in cold frames.

Size H: 3–4 ft.; S: 1½ ft. **Aspect** Sun. **Flowering season** Late summer. **Planting partners** *Phalaris arundinaceae*, *Pontederia cordata*, *Scrophularia auriculata* 'Variegata.'

Lythrum salicaria
(Purple loosestrife)

An excellent wildlife-garden plant whose attractive spikes of bright magenta flowers attract many insects. There are several cultivars in varying shades of pink. The lance-shaped leaves grow in a bushy clump.

Size H: 4–5 ft. **Aspect** Sun or part-shade. **Flowering season** Late summer. **Planting partners** *Eupatorium purpureum*, *Ligularia dentata*.

Meadowsweet
see *Filipendula ulmaria*

Osmunda regalis
(Royal fern)

A stately large fern for the waterside with bright green, leathery, divided fronds that turn a beautiful rusty-red in the autumn. Rusty-brown, fertile flower spikes are produced on the taller fronds when the plant is mature. **Size** H: 5–6 ft.; S: 3 ft. **Aspect** Part-shade. **Flowering season** Grown for its foliage. **Planting partners** *Ligularia dentata, Lysichiton americanus, Primula florindae.*

Plantain lily see *Hosta*

Primula

The following species are ideally suited to the waterside, particularly when massed in bold groups.

Primula beesiana is a vigorous, candelabra-type primula with rough-textured, large, oblong leaves and rich purple flowers which have yellow eyes in tiered whorls. Flower colors vary from pale mauve to deep carmine. **Size** H: 2 ft.; S: 1 ft. **Aspect** Sun or part-shade. **Flowering season** Late spring to early summer. **Planting partners** *Ajuga reptans, Hosta sieboldiana, Iris sibirica.*

P. bulleyana is a candelabra-type primula whose flowers, which have whorls of orange-yellow, grow on strong stalks. The thin, toothed leaves are dark green and oblong- to lance-shaped. **Size** H: 2–3 ft.; S: 1½ ft. **Aspect** Sun or part-shade. **Flowering season** Summer. **Planting partners** *Carex elata* 'Aurea,' *Iris ensata, Lysimachia nummularia.*

P. denticulata is a neat primula and one of the earliest to flower. It has round heads of lilac to rich carmine-red flowers on stout stems and broadly lance-shaped, toothed leaves. Pure white and pink flowers are also available. **Size** H: 9–12 in.; S: 1 ft. **Aspect** Sun. **Flowering season** Early spring. **Planting partners** *Cardamine pratensis, Leucojum aestivum, Primula rosea.*

P. florindae is one of the most vigorous of the waterside primulas with several heads of large, drooping, sulfur-yellow, bell-like flowers covered with farina. The broad, coarse, heart-shaped leaves can reach up to 8 in. long. **Size** H: 2½ ft.; S: 2 ft. **Aspect** Sun or part-shade. **Flowering season** Midsummer. **Planting partners** *Iris ensata, Lysimachia nummularia* 'Aurea,' *Osmunda regalis.*

P. japonica is a reliable and showy form of candelabra primula for massed waterside planting. It has dense tiers of red, white, pink or crimson flowers on stout stems. The large, coarse, lance-shaped leaves are pale green with a bluish tint. 'Miller's Crimson' is dark red while 'Postford White' is an outstandingly beautiful white. **Size** H: 2–3 ft.; S: 1 ft. **Aspect** Sun or part-shade. **Flowering season** Late spring to early summer. **Planting partners** *Ajuga reptans, Hosta sieboldiana, Iris laevigata* 'Variegata.'

Primula japonica

P. prolifera (syn. *P. helodoxa*) is a bold, candelabra-type, yellow-flowered primula which is similar to *P. florindae* but lacks a coating of farina on the tall flower spikes. The long, pale green leaves are oval and toothed. **Size** H: 3 ft.; S: 1½ ft. **Aspect** Sun or part-shade. **Flowering season** Early summer. **Planting partners** *Filipendula ulmaria, Hosta sieboldiana, Iris sibirica.*

P. pulverulenta is one of the most elegant of the candelabra-type primulas. This species has bold tiers of rich-crimson, purple-eyed flowers held on a flower spike covered with farina. The lance-shaped, toothed leaves are

Rheum palmatum
'Atrosanguineum'

slightly smaller and more wrinkled than those of many other candelabra types of primula. The Bartley hybrids provide an excellent pink-flowered selection.

Size H: 2 ft.; S: 1 ft. **Aspect** Sun or part-shade. **Flowering season** Late spring. **Planting partners** *Hosta sieboldiana*, *Iris sibirica*, *Myosotis palustris*.

P. rosea has pink, polyanthus-like flowers on short stems above oval to lance-shaped leaves. The leaves are often flushed with a bronze coloring when young.

Size H: 4–6 in.; S: 6 in. **Aspect** Sun. **Flowering season** Early spring.

Planting partners *Caltha palustris* 'Alba,' *Leucojum vernum*, *Scilla sibirica*.

Purple loosestrife
see *Lythrum salicaria*

Rheum
(Giant rhubarb)

A genus of striking, large-leaved plants of which *R. alexandrae* is the exception in size—the leaves grow to only 3 ft. and the flower spike reaches 4–5 ft. It is as decorative as its larger relatives, with attractively veined, dark green, glossy leaves and cream-colored bracts on the flower spike. *R. palmatum*, the more common and most easily grown species, grows to 6–8 ft. high with large, apple-green, deeply cut leaves and creamy-white flower spikes. 'Atrosanguineum' is similar but has more deeply cut, reddish leaves, particularly on the underside. It also has vivid crimson, fluffy flower spikes.

Size S: 5 ft. **Aspect** Sun or part-shade. **Flowering season** Spring. **Planting partners** Best planted as a single specimen or in groups.

Rodgersia

A genus of handsome plants, grown for their foliage. *R. aesculifolia* has divided, crinkled and bronze-tinted leaves, 1–1½ ft. wide, which resemble those of the horse chestnut tree. The small spikes of white flowers, produced in summer, resemble those of astilbes; *R. podophylla* has palmately divided leaves with

jagged lobes at the edges, which are bronzy when young and grow to 3 ft., turning coppery in the autumn. The creamy-white flowers are held in panicles above the foliage and appear in mid-summer.

Size H and S: 3–4 ft. **Aspect** Part-shade. **Flowering season** Summer. **Planting partners** *Osmunda regalis*; with *Rodgersia aesculifolia*: *Astilbe*, *Filipendula ulmaria*; with *Rodgersia podophylla*: *Iris sibirica*.

Royal fern see *Osmunda regalis*

Trollius

This is a delightful genus of compact, brightly colored plants. *T. × cultorum* is an easily contained group of hybrid waterside plants, growing to 3 ft. tall with a spread of 2 ft. It has a display of orangy-yellow, incurving, globular flowers about 2 in. across and mounds of attractive, dissected leaves. One of the parents, *T. chinensis*, is similar but the flowers contain prominent, narrow stamens. *T. europaeus*, with a height and spread of 2 ft., has cool, lemon-yellow, curved blooms growing above the heavily dissected, buttercup-like foliage.

Aspect Sun or part-shade. **Flowering season** Late spring to early summer. **Planting partners** *Iris pseudacorus* 'Variegata'; with *Trollius × cultorum*: *Hosta undulata* 'Variegata,' *Primula bulleyana*; with *Trollius europaeus*: *Alchemilla mollis*, *Primula japonica*.

Umbrella plant see *Darmera peltata*

Trees and shrubs

Alnus glutinosa
'Aurea'

A slower-growing, smaller form of the common alder with beautiful, bronzy-red catkins and round leaves, yellow when young and paler green in the summer.

Size H: to 80 ft.; S: 30 ft. **Aspect** Sun or part-shade. **Season of interest** Spring.

Blueberry
see *Vaccinium angustifolium*

Cornus

The dogwoods provide interest throughout the seasons, making them valuable near water. *C. alba*, a rampant, shrubby plant, with a height and spread of 10 ft., is shown to best effect if cut back hard every spring. It has blood-red-colored stems in winter with white, blue-tinged, oval fruits. There are several excellent cultivars, including: 'Elegantissima Variegata,' with rich, silver-variegated leaves; 'Gouchaultii' and 'Kesselringii,' both with pinkish leaves margined with yellow; 'Sibirica,' with vivid red stems; and 'Spaethii,' with red stems and handsome green variegated foliage. *C. stolonifera* 'Flaviramea,' a yellow-stemmed, shrubby cultivar, is less vigorous. It grows to a height of 3–4 ft. and has a spread of 3 ft. It is also better for cutting back hard each spring.

Aspect Sun or part-shade. **Season of interest** Winter for stems and bark; summer for variegated and colored foliage.

Dawn redwood see *Metasequoia glyptostroboides*

Metasequoia glyptostroboides
(Dawn redwood)

This conical and moderately fast-growing, deciduous conifer has reddish, fibrous bark which becomes fluted with age. The small, soft young leaves are a refreshing light green and enjoy a brief yellow and orange coloring in autumn before falling. Its narrow habit makes it suitable where space is at a premium.

Size H: 100–115 ft.; S: 20 ft. **Aspect** Sun or part-shade. **Season of interest** Summer and winter; attractive foliage in autumn.

Salix
(Willow)

Several willows are suitable for the sides of medium-sized pools, particularly when they are pruned hard in order to produce vividly colored young wood. *S. alba vitellina*, a form of white willow, is a blaze of color in the winter landscape, where its scarlet-orange branches make a brilliant display. If cut back hard each spring it is manageable and the intensity of the stem colors is enhanced.

Size H: 60–80 ft.; S: 26 ft. **Aspect** Sun. **Season of interest** Winter.

S. caprea 'Kilmarnock' or 'Weeping Sally' is a suitable specimen weeping willow for planting near ponds. The broad, gray-green leaves are oblong and downy when young.

Size H and S: 6½ ft. **Aspect** Sun or

part-shade. **Season of interest** Spring.

S. daphnoides is a handsome species with downy young shoots which become purply with a waxy bloom. It is best cut back in spring to restrict its size and encourage the intensity of the violet stems.

Size H: 30–40 ft.; S: 20 ft. **Aspect** Sun or part-shade. **Season of interest** Winter.

S. lanata is a shrubby species of willow with a soft covering of gray hairs over the buds and young branches. Its leaves are seen to best effect in winter.

Size H: 2–3 ft.; S: 4–5 ft. **Aspect** Full sun. **Season of interest** Spring and winter.

Vaccinium angustifolium
(Blueberry)

This low-growing shrub has edible fruit and narrow, lanceolate leaves borne on twiggy, wiry shoots which turn red in the autumn. The small, red-streaked white flowers are held in racemes above the foliage.

Size H: 3–8 in.; S: 1 ft. **Aspect** Part-shade or sun. **Season of interest** Spring and late summer.

Willow see *Salix*

Although not usually planted right at the water's edge, trees and shrubs shield the water surface from wind, while specimen trees also make appealing reflections.

Index

Page numbers in *italics* refer to illustrations; numbers in **bold** to the chapter on Key Plants.

Plant hardiness zones

This hardiness map will help you to establish which plants are most suitable for your garden. The zones 1–11 are based on the average annual minimum temperature for each zone and appear after the plant entry in the index. The lower number indicates the northernmost zone in which the plant can survive the winter and the higher number the most southerly area in which it will perform consistently.

ZONE 1	BELOW −50° F
ZONE 2	−50° TO −40°
ZONE 3	−40° TO −30°
ZONE 4	−30° TO −20°
ZONE 5	−20° TO −10°
ZONE 6	−10° TO 0°
ZONE 7	0° TO 10°
ZONE 8	10° TO 20°
ZONE 9	20° TO 30°
ZONE 10	30° TO 40°
ZONE 11	ABOVE 40°

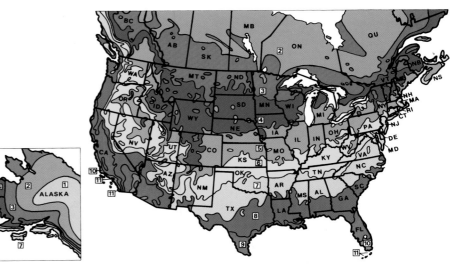